THROUGH PAIN TO FREEDOM

THROUGH PAIN TO FREEDOM

Tom Johanson

Bishopsgate Press Ltd.
37 Union Street, London SE1 1SE

British Library Cataloguing in Publication Data

Johanson, Tom
Through pain to freedom.
1. Spiritual healing
I. Title
615.8′52 BT732.5

ISBN 1-85219-016-7 Pbk

All enquiries and requests relevant to this title should be sent to the publisher, Bishopsgate Press Ltd., 37 Union Street, London SE1 1SE

Printed in Great Britain by
Whitstable Litho Ltd., Whitstable, Kent

CONTENTS

FOREWORD

WHY THIS BOOK WAS WRITTEN

The records of world population tell us that more than 5000 million people live, work, suffer, enjoy and die on this planet of ours. It is estimated that something like 200,000 die each day, but are soon replaced.

This endless movement of human beings has gone on since beyond the reach of memory, and for most of them history has created no record. Frequently the thought arises in the minds of many: 'What has become of the countless, forgotten millions who arrive from nowhere and eventually disappear into the past?' Scientists confidently tell us that nothing can be destroyed but is only transformed. What then has become of those millions of souls who also had their dreams, hopes, fears and the scars of many difficult experiences? Man knows that he is destined to die and will eventually disappear from the eyes of his successors, just as the many millions of souls before him have done. We, also, shall work and struggle to fulfil dreams and for a few years strive to turn hopes into reality until, also, we are absorbed into whatever lies beyond. We live, love, suffer and then die to the world we know – for what plan and what purpose is all this ordered? This the worrying question which continues to haunt mankind.

The answer to this question perhaps evades most people and, yet, there is no question about what all people are seeking. All are seeking some kind of happiness, some kind of peace, or a place of security. The world in which we find ourselves is far from comforting. Eternally troubled by strife, turmoil, wars and greed, may turn in desperation to some religion or other, from one teacher to another, or from one book to another. From time to time man will experience some form of gratification, but is it lasting? Is it totally fulfilling? Inevitably, in time he will realise it falls short of happiness. But, nevertheless, perhaps a little dispirited, he continues to pursue happiness by any way which looks promising. He attends meetings, seeks out teachers, reads numerous books, attends specific groups, always searching for something permanent, something lasting and progressive. He may not be aware of it, but he is instinctively looking for **Reality**. Some enlightened souls have found it; they are referred to as mystics, gurus, masters and evolved teachers. They have had the 'Direct Experience'. They have found the Permanent, the Purpose, the Lasting, the Real. The 'Direct Experience' came not from what others said, not from church teachers, not from some organisation, religious or otherwise, and not from special books; they all tell us they found it **within**.

Therefore, the one who is searching for lasting happiness must search within. But before he can begin this search and achieve the Direct Experience, he must **know** – really know – **himself**. Can he achieve this by listening to what others say or what an author believes and puts into a book? The only reason why he does not **know** himself is because he does not know others. Of course, he knows a lot about other people's ideas, he knows a lot about facts and words which he has gathered from others. This is information gathered from the **outside**. If you are searching for Unchanging Happiness then you must understand something about the thing you are seeking. For instance, what part of you is the Seeker? **What** is the Seeker? **Why** is the Seeker? Truth, that which opens the way to the Direct Experience, which conveys happiness, may be entirely different from the thought – the **Seeker's** idea of happiness. Therefore, it is essential the searcher fully understands the nature of those aspects which he seeks and the essential nature of the subject he is seeking.

Thus we come to a point where we must ask ourselves most earnestly and profoundly if the Truth we are pursuing concerns essentially **ourself** – our **inner** self? Or can the truth we are seeking be revealed to us by someone else, through a particular organisation, religion or through following the words of someone else? These questions bring us back to this principal Truth, 'If we do not first understand ourselves we then do not have any real basis for directive thought, therefore all searches must prove futile, frustrating and entirely in vain'. We can, of course, run away from the whole thing. We can isolate ourselves by inhabiting the top of a mountain and allow all strife, wars and turbulences of the world to go by without touching us. But will that solve anything? Consider the inner aspects of yourself which react to the stress, the fears of war, the turmoil. Would they automatically and totally go away? They are the weaknesses, the areas of ignorance within the soul, which are also the **causes** which prevented you from knowing yourself. They have in fact barricaded you from the Eternal Truth, from the Permanent Happiness. How long can you remain on the mountain, isolated? Sooner or later you must come down and then the same areas of ignorance will return with you. They will react exactly as before, conjuring up the same fears, stress and anxieties. Knowing ourselves not only means recognising the 'why' of our disturbing weaknesses but creating the courage to confront and finally overcoming them.

Man's courage and honest recognition of his soul's weaknesses is the **only** foundation on which he can begin the search for himself. Before he can begin to **know**, first, by overcoming obstacles of his own making, he must know what he **is**. If he is greedy, jealous, vain, selfish and suspicious, these are aspects **he** has created and are not the fault of the society which surrounds him. These basic facts concerning man's ignorance of himself and his futile attachment to outward sources in a vain attempt to find happiness, are the basic reasons why this book was written.

The reader is, I sincerely hope, about to set out on a journey to find Reality, Truth and **Himself**. This cannot be overstressed. Before the Seeker can even begin to understand **where** to start, what he hopes to achieve, how he can recognise the **purpose**, the **how** and the **why** whilst in the society of others, surrounded by books, churches, teachers and unbelievers, he must first begin by understanding **himself**. The sincere searcher is one who is **totally** concerned with initial knowledge of **himself**, and **not** how soon he will arrive and glory in his achievement.

Without knowing yourself, without thoroughly understanding your own way of thinking and therefore acting and reacting, **why** you think as you do about certain things, **why** you have certain beliefs, **why** you react in a particular way to certain people and experiences, how can you think correctly, truly and spiritually about the way ahead, without knowing the **real** substance of your thoughts and the inner-centre from which they came, your search is useless. Thus your actions and reactions will mean nothing, but will probably only add to the struggle. We will simply continue to experience, and mentally react to wars, conflicts, atrocities and other numerous tragedies. We display anger, fear, make judgements and constantly ask the one question, 'Why does God allow this? Before we can begin to understand the reason why, the end-purpose, we must, again, begin with ourselves. We must examine, carefully, our own thoughts and impulses. One has to be extraordinarily alert and constantly analysing. To study oneself is to realise how the thoughts and responses of others operate. Look upon each person's thoughts and actions as a mirror of your own. In time there will develop a greater awareness not only of one's self but of others with whom you have a relationship. To know yourself is to study yourself during every physical and mental action. Great difficulties arise because we have so many commitments, so many responsibilities with the result that we become impatient and irritable. Everywhere, everyone, is the real testing ground. In the kitchen, in the office, the factory, the shop and in the high street. This is where your greatest opportunities for progress lie. These are the ideal places for self-reflection, to study why and observe. Slowly, very slowly, self-knowledge will come and with it more clarity of the purpose of life. However beware, do not look for an ending – there is never an end. But as one studies, observes and reflects upon oneself, one discovers a developing tranquillity. Only in that tranquillity can Reality come into being. Therefore, without this self-knowledge through self-observation, (without relying upon the need to attend meetings, listening to words, reading books) your journey will be futile, a useless activity without meaning.

Finally, it would be wise for the reader to contemplate carefully the following truth. For all your troubles, missed opportunities and heart-breaks, it would be foolish and meaningless to blame your neighbours, your friends and family, or even God. Man creates his own barriers, frustrations and problems. It is a true saying and one worth remembering: 'No one has the power to hurt you unless you first give them the power.' Man has been given complete free will over his own destiny. He can travel as far away from God as he wishes, but God will never lose sight of him.

The world visible and invisible is replete with helpers, inspirers, counsellors and exacting laws all working at all times to guide, uplift and bring their charge back to reality. There are spiritual laws which even put to use the difficult ways and behaviour of your neighbour in order to reveal to you the very same weaknesses within yourself. In effect, difficult people are merely further opportunities for self-reflection, observation and progression. Think of your difficult neighbour as a wonderful teacher and you will discover not only more about yourself but that everything in life is perfectly planned for your ultimate freedom.

INTRODUCTION

The author of a book on philosophy must, I think, necessarily say for whom the book is written and the reader must also be informed how the author acquired his knowledge. A writer cannot devote many years to endeavouring to bring some understanding of the nature of the world, the purpose of human life, the outworking of the many intricate natural and spiritual laws, to the questioning minds of ordinary men and women without knowing something of the dilemmas, fears and questions which haunt their daily lives.

Before the reader jumps to the conclusion that I am being somewhat presumptuous, I would beg his or her indulgence at least until the end of this introduction. Many authors on similar subjects admit to having read widely and investigated painstakingly into the phenomena of inspirational awareness, and the experiences of mystical insight of other persons in order that they may arrive at some reasonable deductions, but have themselves been excluded from any convincing first-hand experiences. Therefore, the authenticity of their records is totally dependent upon the accuracy of the recollections of their informants.

I, therefore, sincerely inform my readers that never at any time have I undertaken any such survey. It is my hope, as we proceed through this book, to prove to every thinking person that there sleeps within each soul a level of awareness which lies beyond the limitations of intellectual reasoning. In other words, a deeper intuitive level, obviously well developed in the poet, meditational teacher and the highly sensitive. As to how this faculty of intuitional insight was first awakened and experienced within myself, I will deal in detail a little later.

The questions which arise in the minds of many and to which I will try to give some meaning are the same ageless questions which return again and again to trouble the thinkers of every generation in spite of countless scripts produced by philosophers, religious teachers and esoteric adepts. These questions revolve around the 'nature of man', 'the purpose of life', 'why man suffers', and 'his ultimate destiny'. Man was born into this world and many complain that they were never consulted and will likewise ultimately be rejected from it without choice. However, once his mind becomes aware of and accepts the tasks confronting him, he gradually becomes conditioned to his environment on three major levels, physical, emotional and intellectual. At first, only to very few does it seriously occur to question why they really exist, what their true nature is, or that of the world, or why there is a world at all. The fact is that once our emotional and intellectual side becomes 'conditioned' to its environment it naturally accepts the struggle, the pain and the interminable feeling of 'wanting'. This is the natural law's merciful provision to allow us to secure as harmonious and reasonably balanced correspondence as possible with our environment. Though never meant to be a perfect existence – impossible because of its very nature – nevertheless, a reasonably enjoyable earth-life can be secured.

This process of 'conditioning' or 'adaptation to environment' provides the necessary experiences of the 'opposites' to secure the soul's progress and ultimate release from the frustrating limitations of the physical environment. As the reader progresses through these pages it will, I hope, be made clear that his **entire** progress is solely dependent on the stimulus that produces all disharmonies. At first, and for a long time, the operative life in the physical world directs its inhabitants to live *against* the natural spiritual flow and unwittingly create physical 'self-centres' of interest and 'self-activity'. From within these centres disharmonies arise which frequently and effectively trouble not only the persons in them but also the environment itself. This emotionally and intellectually planned process, no matter how uncomfortable and disturbing it may be, eventually helps us to become wise enough and courageous enough to accept it as nothing more than a series of opportunities to further our progress.

How far are we left alone to achieve any degree of progress? What is the philosophy of accident? Considering the many seemingly inequalities in life, the crippled and the healthy, the handsome and the ugly, the intelligent and the backward, could it be that we are just playthings on the chessboard of destiny? Let the reader look back reflectively over his own life and note how many times a particular turning or new way of life was determined by what he assumed was 'mere chance', an 'accident', 'spot of good luck', or a 'chance meeting'? Looking back over my own life and reflecting upon one incredible experience which completely changed my thinking and way of life, I have described it thus: 'an extremely High Spiritual Order seemed to touch **all** levels of the lower-self and creatively transform them.' Concerning many such mystical happenings, or Supreme Interventions, which have dramatically transformed the way of life for many, John Buchan has said, 'I do not for one moment argue that these incomprehensible events are incapable of rationalisation by some Higher Intelligence than our own; I can only say that we cannot fit them into any mortal scheme of effects and schemes.'

I now invite the reader to consider the strangeness of my own personal experience which, I believe, not only touched upon the inspirational and intuitive but also awakened what I can only describe as mystical insight. It began in the autumn of 1949, the year when my wife and child decided to leave England and take up a new life in Canada. Because of some strange, compelling inner conviction I stayed behind. The years that followed were long, empty and extremely lonely. Frequent, intruding thoughts concerning my future merely added to the misery, the hopelessness and to the depth and frequency of bouts of depression. My obsessive desire for the ultimate release grew with each day, but the end of life seemed impossibly far away.

During the summer of 1956 the events of life took on an unexpected and a more promising turn. Through chance, accident, good luck, or by a 'planned' act a companion entered my life. She was gentle, spiritually minded and fun-loving. For three short years life was idyllic. Like the awakening of a beautiful spring after a long harsh winter, my life was beginning to warm with the promise of a new life. Once more I was filled with hope and the zeal to fulfil long-forgotten ambitions. Then on Thursday, 3 September 1959 the cruel shutters of fate came crashing down, obliterating a promising future full of hope and exciting dreams. My friend died of cancer at the age of thirty-three years. Mercifully, like an answer to a prayer, there came during this desolate, benumbing time a comrade to give much needed comfort and support. He was a monk who some years previously had given up his monastic life to work among the townsfolk as a healer and counsellor. Without overtures or explanations he immediately packed me into a taxi and took me to his home, a secluded house situated at the bottom of a beautiful hill. For two days and two nights I experienced crushing grief and loneliness. Then two days later it happened. During the late afternoon of Saturday, 5 September, sitting alone in the lounge of my friend's home, an elderly lady neighbour came in to talk to me.

'It is a beautiful, quiet evening', she said, 'let us go for a short walk.' Not caring what I did and without comment I left the house with her. The road was strangely quiet and empty which accentuated my feelings of loneliness and sadness. My companion continued to talk but I failed to register any meaning in her words. I was locked away in my own private world of sorrow which was crowded with torturing memories. When **that** feeling actually started I do not know. It was just there, an incongruous calmness. No longer were there feelings of grief or sadness, not even a feeling of loss. It was as if I had just walked out of a dark, terrifying storm and now it had suddenly stopped. Everything was light again, calm and soothing. There was a strange silence, no sounds from the street or from the mouth of my companion. Even our footsteps gave off no sound. I heard myself say, or was it just a thought, 'I must return to my room now.'

Back in my room I lay down on the bed fully clothed. **That** strange total feeling of tranquillity and calmness mercifully remained with me. Then slowly I found myself being gently enfolded in a cloud of pure silver which seemed to grow and reach infinite immensities of brilliant light, yet there was no dazzling effect. Next there slowly developed within me a deeper understanding of everything I was now sensitive to **all** things – to the entire universe which lay beyond my four walls, but which no longer existed. The light seemed to grow brighter and more pure. It appeared to come from some distant sun and yet, at the same time, it was still within the centre of myself. The light, inexplicably, seemed to grow even more pure penetrating every cell of my body and even beyond that. Slowly all around me was transformed into a golden glory and **I** was the immense sun of brilliance and, yet, the sun was the universe and **all** that reached beyond it. Never once did I cease to be myself and yet I was not **one**. Directly afterwards (or was it at the same time?) there came an infinite sense of exultation, indescribable, immense joyousness followed by an illumination of what I can only describe as the Christ Splendour. This has ever since been an inseparable part of my awareness and has directed and inspired my life. It seemed as if the eyes of the soul were opened and I became the ineffable fullness of the Cosmic Spirit, and, yet, at the same time, **became** the fullness of Divine Wisdom. I felt I understood the whole world both here and beyond. I felt I had found a great discovery and, yet, the discovery was **myself**!

Throughout this experience time had ceased. There was only a pure level of silence beneath all sound. If time was passing then it was of another dimension where consciousness as we knew it did not exist. Everything was amazingly lucid. This, I knew, **was** another world – the **real** world where the logical mind, like a sack, endlessly collecting events, incidents, purposes and desires, was lost in the realm of illusion. This was the timeless world where everything was of a different dimension, where everything was of an unchanging beauty – this was the world of reality, and yet it was still **myself**! If there was anything I felt, or heard, it was the **message,** 'Truth and Love are One and the only approach is **suffering**.' With that I dropped into the sleep of the mortal.

Next morning after I awoke I no longer beheld the Power –

yet it had still left **something**. That something still remains with me to this day. I still remember all and realise that I had glimpsed a world beyond our world of earth-day life. The latter, when compared, is unreal and dead. The experience I have presented clearly indicated 'levels' of worlds which gradually and inexorably approach closer and closer to the Reality, yet it would be impossible to say where one world of significance ends and another begins. I realised only too clearly that it is the purpose of mankind to traverse and experience each and every level. As the soul proceeds, the feeling of unreality becomes less and less, finally deepening to mystical awareness when the Self finds itself in a world of **Being** rather than of **Becoming**.

During the extremely sensitive days that followed I felt I had lost my sense of separateness and individuality, that is, I had discovered and experienced a True Self. I was at one with all souls and felt in the presence of some divine being. However, such experiences cannot be sustained for long nor can they be commanded. It was as though, for a while, I had gained access to the Inner Citadel of the Higher Self and experienced its glory. Also, without a doubt, it revealed a promise to man, the pilgrim, exiled in a world of time, limitation and illusion. One day he will attain this glory but only through struggle, suffering and seeking.

When I look back I **know** something had happened to me. I knew I had made some profound discovery. I asked myself, 'Can this be the mystery of life'? All I know is that I am no longer the 'I' I thought I was. Now I **know** there is no death. I thought of the peace, the peace that passed beyond all my understanding, and yet I felt so unworthy. Only hours after that unforgettable experience I was seized with the desire to write. Every bit of paper was collected and as strange, but exciting truths filled my mind they were immediately committed to paper. Page after page was filled with the reason for suffering, the nature of the world, the nature of man, the purpose of Jesus and the attainment of Christhood. It was like remembering ancient, long forgotten secrets, but I **knew** they were truths. Flash after flash presented to my consciousness a clear outline of the meaning and purpose of the way of man. Each impression was a shining presence. I saw that the life in man is eternal as all life is eternal and that the soul of man is as immortal as that of God. All this and much more was tirelessly conveyed to bits of paper, empty confectionery bags, opened-up cigarette packets.

Thus the early days of my discovery passed, but they were not easy days. Feelings of intense sensitivity stayed with me making a normal day difficult. The sound of moving vehicles, aeroplanes and people was very painful. Even in the home of my friend, the monk, I tried to avoid conversation. Desperately I needed to be alone, secluded from all aspects of civilisation. But later even my quiet meditative moments became times of great distress. Suddenly various incidents which I had long forgotten thrust themselves into my mind; distressing things. I relived personal acts of callousness, cruelty, anger, dishonesty, selfishness and thoughtlessness. These past incidents of my life became more and more frequent, more disturbing, even crucifying. These memories were never of the good times, only the selfish acts. With each memory the feelings of remorse became more intense. I did not see God's purpose in these acts only His intent relentlessness to fulfil his purpose whatever it was. As the days passed it seemed that the whole of the unworthy side of my life had seeped into my mind. Many times I pondered on the meaning of these experiences of seemingly meaningless distress? All the things I suffered were from the past. Did God, in spite of my cruel loss, think no more of me than a man who had cut down a tree for fuel? In spite of those thoughts I still believed there was a purpose behind all things, even my moments of distress. All mystics, I recalled, had discovered that behind the world of ordinary earth-day life there were other worlds of being which, when compared with the former, were real and indescribably alive. Surely, I thought, it must be the same with our own **inner** worlds of Self. There must be many such inner worlds or levels of consciousness, of an ever closer approach to reality. Records of mystics show us that there are depths or levels of the ego-self which serve as veils between it and the Absolute Self. These veils constitute collectively the ego-personality which ordinary people believe themselves to be – the 'reality' with which they identify themselves. There are exalted beings who have achieved full enlightenment; they are the beings who can at will withdraw the veils from the light of Reality. Others who do not yet have a fully conscious knowledge of the unity of the ego-self with the Absolute Self are not aware of the existence of the veils and so continue to live a life of self delusionment. When we are able to analyse what 'self-delusion' means our thoughts turn to a belief in 'possessiveness' and a wish-fulfilment type of belief in the need for the accumulation of things and valuables. This is the level which believes that protection of 'ownership', whether by anger, threat or strength, is fully justified. The more I contemplated my mystical experience, the more I wondered if man himself could **do** anything to achieve **the** experience. Obviously the truest answer must be that whilst this experience is beyond the normal ego-self, nevertheless, if man were to fulfil certain conditions then the experience is a possibility. The only condition must be complete abstinence from preoccupation with the 'sense' objects of the world. Then I remembered that the Christian Order has its own demand for the 'Way' – **purgation is a moral purification.** Again I remembered reading somewhere the words of Sri Krishna, 'Progress is made through pain.' True self and Divine-Self are one; to **know** the **measure** is **suffering**. In terms of my simile of the many veils round the Absolute Self it seemed to me that these veils had slowly become thin and dissolved away into a deepening mystical experience. The final and searing revelations from my past life **incidents** was, I believe, a form of purgation or moral purification. It seemed to me that the outer mind had had access, for a moment, to the Inner-Self and seen its glory. I had discovered myself as I **am**, not as I thought I was. The essence of the experience was the glimpsing of the true Self **by** the Ego and in this experience we come to know for a moment our true divine nature. The experience was so overwhelming and wondrous that, as the reader will have seen by my struggle to describe it, any language will fail to capture it fully.

Man is not always aware of the cry from the heart for the

Eternal; the hunger of the soul for God, but the cry is often answered when we are at our lowest ebb, then there is total hopelessness, or when we think all is lost. The interpretation I made of my spiritual experience not only revealed my frequent betrayals of the Spirit, but gave me a glimpse of the goal. Now I have to be prepared for the Way to it. The major problem standing in the path was first the need to realise, not in theory, but by practical experience, that the ego-mind, or earth-mind, by which I had always identified myself was not the True-Self. The ego-mind is **conditioned** by its immediate environment. An environment compiled by possessiveness, desire, fear, frustration, anger and jealousy. These conditions are accepted by the mind and its judgement is considered of correct value.

If the mind should receive from the spiritual level, as often happens, a quota of intuitive knowledge – or Truth – it may be asked why such wisdom is not immediately recognised and acted upon. The principal cause is the distorting mechanism of the **conditioned** mind. Truth cannot filter through a conditioned mind without suffering a considerable degree of distortion. That is why honest and even sincere people make many differing judgements of different values. Their decisions and consequent actions are all too often 'coloured' by a sense of personal justification or righteousness. The feelings and emotions that support these preconceptions are retained and even added to, and so the environment continues to condition the mind. The mind continues to be the suffering slave of the environment until it learns to understand the nature of selfishness, greed, desire or, alternatively, to understand the **origin** of love, goodness and self-sacrifice. The destined ultimate function of the mind is to express Wisdom of the Highest Order and to learn how to influence and control the lower levels of mind. Alas, it is the Law that, during man's initial stages of progress, he must first experience – therefore suffer – the limitations and illusions of the lower levels of mind.

I have written this introductory chapter to give some meaning to the way man must take in his spiritual questing. It can be described as the final achievement of a new state of consciousness, such as the high mystical state I had glimpsed, but could not sustain. I know now that the ego-mind must be totally surrendered in such experiences. In other words, total surrender means total self-sacrifice which cannot be undertaken without experiencing considerable pain – the pain of knowing what we **were**. Once the mind is awakened from its preconditioned state it is shocked by the things it took for granted. My own reactions were of unbearable remorse. At the time I thought the vividness of the 'recalls' were unnecessarily cruel, harsh and remorseless. Later, much later, I saw what the revelations were trying to do. With all their power they were trying to make me change course, to bend the line of my thinking, but it hurt me more than I have ever been hurt. At the acutest point, when I thought I could no longer retain my sanity, I **realised – I saw.** I understood the nature of the acts committed during moments of spiritual ignorance, of selfishness, thoughtlessness, total sensuality; things I had forgotten, but still retained in the warp of the soul. This was the moment of purgation, the moral purification, the renunciation of the love of gain, love of fame or love of pleasure.

I think it may be helpful to the reader for me to relate a particular agonising experience. In my room (in the monk's home) there was an unusual and uniquely expressive painting of the face of Christ. It was my unfailing duty every morning to kneel and pray before that image. One particular morning (whilst I was going through my period of renunciation or time of painful recalls) as I knelt in prayer I clearly heard the words, 'But Jesus was only a man'. Panic filled my soul – my last thread of hope was gone. In great fear I cried out, 'you have already taken the one great joy out of my life, don't destroy the one last hope I have left.' To cling to a belief in Jesus was to cling to the one hope that my friend still lived. I fled from the house with the feeling of being totally lost, desperate, as a suffocating panic possessed my mind. I raced for the solitude and isolation of a small cemetery situated at the top of a beautiful green hill. This was the place I had spent all my days since the passing of my friend. Inwardly, I was tortured by a deeper, more profound feeling of loneliness, the soul craving for some small measure of comfort. Never before in my life had I experienced such depths of helplessness. Silently, I screamed out for **something** to help, I knew not what it was, but I knew it could not be of the earth. I seemed to be under the unending grinding feet of God because again and again those dreaded words went remorselessly around my head, 'Jesus was only a man.' The words would not let me go and yet I **knew** there **must** be an answer. As I sat hunched up, tormented, on the side of the hill, I suddenly understood the Cause, or whatever the power was which was trying to get me to change the course of my thinking – to cut the strings which for too long had tied me to the stake of logic. The strings could only be cut by pain. Pains which hurt me more than I had ever been hurt before. Then I understood. Jesus **was** a man, as I am a man. He had suffered and feared as I and **all** men had feared. He was crucified as all men will be crucified. Christ was not the man, but the **achievement** – the **release** of the soul from its earthly bondage. **This** is what it all meant – **this** was the conversion the pain had been designing. During the pain and the sense of loss I could not see God's purpose but only felt His intent, His entire relentlessness towards His purpose.

I (as are **all** men) was the Jesus, the suffering, the struggle, the pain. Man was being relentlessly pushed down the long difficult road towards the **Christhood – the Realisation of Self**! The hard road had meaning and purpose; it was the **only** way. The road **was** illusion and limitation. To **know** it, to **experience** it, to **suffer** it – was to **know**, to **become** the **infinite** Self. Many times before **the** experience I had attempted various techniques of meditation, but without success. Like a sailing vessel without rudder or sails I had no sense of guidance or idea of the direction to take and even less knowledge of what I was supposed to experience. At least the exercise taught me the futility of trying to force myself along a road for which, either by temperament or spiritual growth, I was not yet ready. In time I did realise that it is totally impossible for anyone to meditate on the deeper mysteries of the human soul without an overwhelming experience which takes one beyond the limitations of the finite mind. The achievement of a new state, or quality, of consciousness such as I had glimpsed during the intensified perceptive splendour, presented me with a perfectly clear concept of the meaning and the way of the human soul, the nature and the path of the universe. From that moment onward the meaning and purpose of meditation became clear and illumined so that doubts and problems no longer existed. Although, I must add, the meaning and the purpose were not an intellectual formulation. Furthermore, at all times during my hours of meditation I was conscious of a strong, almost physical, presence which conveyed not only a sense of union with someone far greater advanced than myself, but a form of communication which, though silent, was unmistakable in its meaning and purpose. Such was my affinity with the enlightened messenger of the other world then, so it remains equally strong and unbroken to this day. With each sitting there is presented to my consciousness a clear concept of the meaning, purpose and the way of humanity. I see that the life in man is eternal as **all** life is eternal, that the soul of man is immortal as God is. I see that the Cosmos, which to the earth-conscious mind is dead matter, is in very truth a **living** presence.

Many times I have looked back over the dark years of my life, the times of loneliness, depression, fear, pain and hopelessness and I realise **this** is what it has all meant, **this** was the achievement it had all been contributing to. I have never claimed to have seen God, but I felt His entire relentlessness towards His purpose. I believe that during those dark years I had served God more meaningfully, more directly, more purely than I have ever done in my life before. My suffering was the means of His achieving. I give the reader these words as they come to me for him to accept or reject as he chooses, but before the decision is reached first consider the words of that great prophet and mystic, Radhakrishnan,

‘The oldest wisdom in the world
tells us that we can consciously unite
with the divine while in the body, for
this is man really born. If he misses
his destiny Nature is not in a hurry; she
will catch up someday and compel him to
fulfil her secret purpose.’

Tom Johanson

CHAPTER ONE

REASON CANNOT EXPLAIN **WHY**

Reason, in spite of the great powers logicians and statisticians have attributed to it, has had no great success in illuminating man's most troublesome questions, 'Why are we here'? 'What is the purpose of life'? Why is there so much suffering, so many disasters in the world'? Why am I'?

To **know** is to **feel** meaning in a purpose. Not simply to believe, not just to hope, or to be told to have faith, but to have a **living** belief in something. This is the assurance and security for which man is forever searching. No doubt these thoughts interest the great philosophers to whom such questions are central to all their thinking and living and, no doubt, many provide trustworthy, wholly satisfying answers, but only for those whom we refer to as the 'enlightened'. I therefore embark upon this book in the hope that it will offer some hope and provide some answers for the many 'unenlightened' who are constantly troubled not merely by their discontent of thought but by the seemingly unending struggle against insecurity, suffering and tragedy. Also those who are confused and resentful of the many gross inequalities affecting individuals. The one recurring disturbing thought which often arises in the mind is, 'Is there one Cosmic Moral Law, and is it fundamentally just and impartial to every individual, or is life simply a whirligig of chance or an existence of haphazard experiences?

Of the greatest part of humanity it can be said they spend all their lives seeking happiness or power or lusting after action of every kind. Concerning many of these their lives are caught up in a pattern not always of their own choosing, but, nevertheless, one from which they can find no way of escape. Their minds have become conditioned by a mixture of ambition, opportunities and environment which they have never seriously questioned or analysed, but they continue to be drawn compulsively along by hope and a desperate desire for security and happiness. Throughout this endless onrush of human effort very few ever find it simply because they do not know how to find it and are totally blind as to where to look, but, much more significantly, they are also totally blind to the **kind** of happiness they should be seeking.

To write about different kinds of happiness may be confusing to the reader. To experience **true** happiness is to understand fully the **true** nature of man and the **true** nature of the world in which he lives. True happiness can never be spasmodic, momentary or fragmented. True, or spiritual, happiness is a totality. First, let us start with the nature of man. Man is Mind, an extremely complex instrument which reaches from infinite heights down to lower reaches, or stratas, which are closely linked with physical-body levels. For reasons which will be revealed as we progress through these pages, the whole of man's endeavours are devoted to and concentrated upon preserving or improving his relationship with his surroundings. These efforts totally dominate the lower emotional and intellectual levels. The process of 'conditioning' or 'adaptation to environment' is only operative below the levels of 'higher' orders of mind. This biological unity provides man with a means of experiencing temporal or spasmodic happiness, but it also prevents him from achieving the unchanging, harmonious **real** Self. This self alone has freedom from the constant demands for things and sensations, but gets little chance to exercise it because of the dominant ego-self or earth-mind. The ego is that centre of the lower mind with which we falsely identify ourselves. This is the 'store-house' of all patterns of thought, desire and experience we have built up throughout our life.

The ego-mind can only recognise those things which offer **temporal** experiences. Therefore it can only accept that which comes in 'instalments'. It recognises only in 'parts' but the **whole** is totally beyond it. The consequences are that when we hold on to this mind, we blindly become prisoners of our habits, fears, desires, hopes and ambitions. In truth we become totally confined to a limited pattern of thought, prejudices, specific teachings, mental limitations and established religious, political and philosophical beliefs. Everyone cherishes the dream of unchanging happiness, total security and freedom from want, but would be highly offended if told that they are their **own** gaolers, responsible for the creation of their own barriers to freedom and therefore happiness. The ego-mind alone creates the confining, imprisoning routines by way of its limited reasoning, intellectual analyses and its close interaction with the physical, emotional and sensual world. The short-lived, never fully satisfying daily routines are of man's own choosing, from which he cannot escape because he does not know how to understand or analyse the nature of his environment. Most believe that it could not be substantially other than it appears to be. Once man learns that in this world he is fettered and later crucified by physically satisfying actions done to appease himself then, and only then, will he be freed from a life which appears largely an endless round of futility and effort.

Previously I wrote about the need for man to understand – to **know** – the true nature of man and the nature of the world. Concerning this statement many would smile in disbelief and turn away, believing that they already understand the basic nature of man and the world. For the largest part of humanity this truth lies completely hidden because they have yet to realise that the vital causes of their bondage remain totally within their own minds – **never outside of them.** Let us begin with the nature of the world, the same world which the great masters and mystics referred to as the **illusionary** world. They did not imply that it was a kind of dream world which did not exist except in our imagination. For those who are ignorant of the **true** nature of man and his purpose in it, **all** things are real and permanent. The ignorant take the entire physical world for granted. They refuse to believe it is anything else but what they see, feel, taste, hear and smell. They love the sensual life, but fear and hate the thought of death. They cling thirstily to the pleasurable and complain about the painful. They frequently experience pessimism, frustration and self-pity. They constantly brood over past mistakes and failures, achieving some relief only when they dream about a better future which never comes. The outside world is a collection of **things** which man desires in order to satisfy a particular craving, be it for food, drink, drugs, clothes, vehicles, wealth, premises, ambition, power or authority. Man slaves daily to acquire the 'things' of the world in order that he may extract sensual experience from them. The mind of man is a collection of **feelings** and memories of past experiences. The spiritually enlightened person recognises that each 'thing' affords a short, limited quota of experience which then becomes extinct once the quota of experience is extracted. The object which once contained the experience must be replaced, not once but an infinite number of times because the experience leaves behind an indelible memory of itself. This memory is the demanding ego and man becomes its slave and has been so for many lives. The ego-mind is old dead material. Mind means memory, therefore by its very nature it can never be new. Memory means the **known**, so how can the known be new? Mind is the past, therefore all that it carries is old and dead. The ego-mind cannot be original, it can only be repetitive. So mind goes on repeating old, dead materialistic thoughts in a thousand different ways. It will replace old with new words, but the **things** and their limited experiences will remain the same. Mind cannot come to **know** the new, the original, because it is the past, while the original is the **Now**, the new. To become the **Now** the old mind has to be put aside to allow the highest consciousness of the **innermost** source to manifest. This is the reality. You are the reality **now**, you have always been the reality but between you and this ultimate awareness there has always been the old mind with its long-dead material. The mind has always jumped in and given its own meaning, its own interpretation. The mind has created the rules of society, the rules of religion, the rules of government, the rules of war and enterprise. Whatever is created by the mind will always be against the New. The New is the infinite, innermost reality, the

Self, the **Spirit**. The Self puts the old mind aside. You are able to look at the world in new colours. An ordinary flower becomes an entire universe, carrying the whole glory of the Divine. Every word takes on a new meaning as if the whole Truth is revealed through it. Everything and anything immediately changes.

Whilst accepting that mind, even on physically connected levels, is the extremely complex instrument of man, reason and logic are regarded as two of its most influential and highest functions. The entire field of physical science bears testimony to this. Reason or logic cannot tell us anything about the nature of consciousness or spirituality. Reason and logic when applied to biological fields, physics and chemistry have achieved phenomenal success on their **own level**, but concerning the fundamental purpose of life, the phenomena of existence, the purpose of consciousness, there remains, and there always will remain, an impenetrable hard core of mystery, totally unintelligible to the mind of reason. Reason is capable of gathering knowledge and information but finds it impossible to explain **why** man thirsts for Truth. The reason-mind cannot understand or describe the source of inspiration or intuition. It cannot explain love or the centre from which it is created or why it springs forth. It cannot describe the nature of colour, only the **vehicle** which conveys the phenomenon, such as the vase, the flower, the wall, the material, the flesh, but it cannot fathom the **source**. It cannot define why beauty exists, or the power of love, kindness and compassion. Admittedly, the reason-mind possesses the remarkable power to create and interpret knowledge derived from results gained from experimental observation. It can formulate techniques of logic and mathmetics which, when applied to our physical world, afford us a cleaner, more orderly and comfortable environment. It can give 'pattern' to the motions of the planets around the sun, provide a simplified hypothesis of the law of gravity, but it cannot explain **why there is a law of gravity**.

We can accord then, to the mind and its function of reason, a power to **discover** the multifarious laws of nature and an ability to experiment in order to manipulate cause and effect. It can discern relationships between various reactions, collate information and apply its findings for the betterment of the community, but it can only operate and discover these truths because the basic ingredients and resultant phenomena are **already** there. It cannot explain **why** they are there. Reason-mind is fully capable of 'clothing' its observations in intelligible form and harnessing the information gathered, but it is only a donkey following a carrot which someone else has placed before it. The 'clothing' may be in words, music, colour or any other artistic impression. Therefore, such is the enormous capacity of reason-mind to discover, to interpret and to manipulate available symbols and phenomena, but its capacity to explain **how** or **why** they are there is totally non-existent.

We have seen, then, how mind, in its function of reason, can answer many questions about our *outside* world, but is totally powerless to answer man's most troublesome questions, 'What are we?' 'Why are we?' 'What is our purpose?' Reason looks upon such questions as indefinables, therefore of no concern. Man is often inspired to create a poem, a concerto or a work of art, he continues to breath rhythmically and the fourteen thousand million cells comprising his body continue to break down, but are immediately repaired or rebuilt – all without the help of the reasoning mind.

When we turn to the most significant emotions, thoughts and ideals in human life – to the appreciation of beauty; the joy of love; sudden inspirations which have borne great works of art; the gifts of truth as expressed by the masters and mystics of philosophy, the simple kindness of a humble soul, we **must** see that there is a **higher** significant level of mind where the true form of **Spirit** shines through and reveals man as the Absolute Reality. There are increasing numbers of people already thirsting for truth, tired and frustrated by the limitations of their physical environment, becoming increasingly dissatisfied with doctrines of belief and systems of reason, but attachment to these systems can only be transcended by a radical turn-about of their thinking and the direction of their searching. Man must cease to look **outwards**. For too long he has looked to and relied upon the resources of the outward, sensational world. This world is entirely dependent upon the maintenance of the sense of possessiveness. Everyone strives to establish things as 'theirs'. With nearly every transaction doubt and fear are usually at the back of the mind - the possible fear of not possessing. Even when possession exists the fear of losing takes its place. When these two basic fears take control of the mind the way is prepared for other fears to germinate, such as jealousy. envy, greed, suspicion, distrust, selfishness and even hate. No love is shown here. As the sense of possessiveness becomes more and more dominant, so the fears and conflicts go on growing more and more. When such a person loves another person, possession eventually takes the place of love. A wife can become a fear, a husband can become a fear, because at any moment either can leave and each is powerless to do anything about it. This is the fear. Should one partner move away, the other's pride, ego and sense of possessiveness is shattered. Life becomes dead, meaningless and dispirited. The more this experience is repeated, the more possessive one becomes. Possessiveness is sometimes mistaken for protectiveness and so more and more walls are created around something that is believed to be love. It becomes a vicious circle and so life becomes a prison. This is not an uncommon way of the outer world. In many ways, concerning things, people and ambitions, we create prisons for ourselves. The **real** life becomes less and less, love slowly disappears because we become more and more afraid that something **might** happen to our possessions or to the persons we love. Then we need more and bigger prisons and this is accomplished in a number of subtle ways - jealousy creates jealousy, possessiveness strengthens possessiveness and other lower emotions are created. Eventually persons are no longer seen as persons but become **things** because a thing can be possessed more easily than a person. A person can only remain a person through love. If you must possess a person, then you must let go of love, but the moment you forego love you kill the glory, the beauty, the warmth, because a **thing** can never respond.

Possessiveness, jealousy, pride, selfishness, greed, suspicion, doubt, distrust and envy create a wall which separates the Wisdom of Spirit from the sensual demands of the ego; Spiritual Freedom from the mind's desire for power; the dignity of the Divine Human Being from the herd instinct of the masses; a belief in the Higher Destiny of Man from the belief in material prosperity by possessiveness. This dividing wall, the encircling periphery, is man's own ego and no one can be as dangerous a gaoler as the ego. Nothing can make man so blind, so short-sighted as the ego and no one can lead man to pain, fear and illusion as can the ego. The ego is terrified of death. It does not understand death because the ego is the periphery and death only takes place on the periphery. Death does not kill, it only kills the ego. It kills the 'tomorrow' mind. Tomorrow is the illusion; it does not exist. The tomorrow-mind puts all difficult things off to a time which does not exist.

Life is an eternal continuum. It never began and it never goes. Only the body has a beginning, has been born therefore only the body can die. But Life, the vital energy, the Spirit, the Soul, the Consciousness which, for a time, inhabits the body, has **never** been born and therefore cannot die. When man dies he simply becomes a **witness** to the body dying. For example, if you move house this is not thought of as a birth or a death, it is just a change of environment. The house changes, but you remain the same. Death is simply something that happens to the wall, the periphery. The difficulties and the pains of life are created for one single purpose, to bring death to the wall so that the Innermost Self can be freed. Always the demolition is painful, frightening, often crucifying. But, in truth, death is but a passing – a passing from the outside to the inside and so to freedom.

In the next chapter I will deal with the nature of the wall and the ways of its destruction.

CHAPTER TWO

THE EGO-WALL

The ultimate function of the higher levels of mind is to reflect the wisdom of the highest spiritual aspects of ourselves. We have already seen how mind on the lower levels can explain many things concerning the physical state, but that it is totally powerless to answer those constantly nagging questions concerning life's purpose to which we are the most eager and hungry to find answers. Mind can **read** about enlightenment and about the ultimate state, it will even fool itself into believing that everything has been understood, but enlightenment and the ultimate are not states which one can **understand**. They are beyond the faculty of understanding. Even if one read everything available about enlightenment, about the ultimate, one would never by this approach **know** anything about these states. Enlightenment is not something you **know about**. To know about something, anything, means that one has collected **knowledge**. All knowledge, is collected by the mind of reason or logic This mind is forever attached to the outside phenomenal world. – The world of logic, opinions, ideas, mixed values, intellectual formulations and a miscellany of personal judgement values. It is of the utmost importance to distinguish between **intellectual** formulations of religion, the essence of spiritual experience, or revelation which is mystical. But all genuine progression depends on the individual's intensive efforts or his endless seeking after endless Truth.

The fact is that objective formulations of religious facts can never be a substitute for experiencing spiritual truth **within** oneself. These formulations are part of all the scriptures throughout the world and should only be considered as general guidelines or signposts for the enquiring mind. But no belief or information on historical religious experiences or events has the power to awaken the mind or soul at the high levels which a spiritual experience or enlightenment can be experienced. Somewhere in our long past we have all made essential discoveries of Truth. It has been stored away at a level where no wisdom is ever lost and at a chance stimulus from a spoken word, a book or during a moment of contemplation, coinciding with a favourable state of mind, a spontaneous response will flash into the mind as something you have already **known**. This is a mystical experience. It should be remembered that there is a vital difference between knowledge and an intuitive, or spiritual, revelation.

Consider the experience of enlightenment as being the absolute manifestion, or expression, of the highest level of your **inner** self. This enlightenment **is** you. How then can one read about '**knowing about**' enlightenment when enlightenment is essentially the state of 'being' - **your** personal experience? Think again. If a person is determined to **know about** enlightenment, where do they begin? With the Bible, Koran, the Bhagavad Gita, or a teacher? All these things belong to the outside. But they can only be interpreted by the reason or the logical mind. These scriptures are truths, but it needs the insight of a great soul and the essence of a mystical, or spiritual experience to recognise the Truth.

One of our greatest poets, Robert Browning and a great mystic once wrote:

> Truth is within ourselves; It takes no rise
> From outward things, whatever you may believe.
> There is an inmost centre in us all
> Where Truth abides in fulness; and around
> Wall upon wall, the gross flesh hems it in
> This perfect, clear perception - which is Truth.

His reference to 'wall upon wall, the gross flesh hems it in' confirms the mystic's belief that matter is only the outside which is controlled and influenced by reason or the logical mind. Truth is the centre hemmed in by walls of matter, logic, reason, information and knowledge. The outside is but a circle; like a wheel it goes round and round forever. It demonstrates continuous movement, but a movement that always arrives back at its beginning. When the masters and mystics referred to the outside world of matter as the place of illusion, they were describing the movement of the wheel. The unenlightened, or materially attached, person experiences a great illusion because though he has the feeling he is moving forward, he is in fact, not going anywhere. He is moving in circles. He is standing still. The unenlightened soul is very much like a little mouse in a big wheel. Its legs are moving faster and faster, the floor of the wheel continues to speed by and the mouse believes it is progressing whereas, in reality, it is standing still. There exists a state of attachment in the mind of the mouse. Movement is physically living. Living is constantly searching for some 'things'. Maybe the mouse is afraid and it is hoping to escape from physical exposure or danger. But it is not moving, even though it believes it is. Does it hope to find a piece of food? Food is life. Little does it realise that even if it finds a piece of food, this will soon be eaten. Then it must find another piece of food, then another and another. The effort is endless. The first piece of food, or the experience, is soon forgotten. The mind is immediately thinking about the next piece of food, after that the next piece and so on. Nothing permanent has been achieved; we have remained at the same spot. The mouse never arrives. The unenlightened man occupies exactly the same rotary world. He moves and moves and moves and reaches nowhere. Yet he feels he is reaching somewhere because he is moving, Man never recognises, never sees, the circle because he can only see a very small part of it. So he only sees a way that is stretching ahead. This is the way the mind of reason and logic works. The man is attached to the circle, but he cannot see the bends.

The circle, or the ego wall; is the cumulation of all desires, ambitions, knowledge of matter. It is also the centre for all possessive emotions such as jealousy, envy, greed, possessiveness, hate, selfishness, suspicion and anger. The ego-wall can only recognise itself which means an acceptance and therefore an attachment to all **things** which are matter. The ego-wall believes these things are reality and that they are necessary for its existence, just as the mouse in the wheel believes that the wheel movement is vital for its life. In one way this is perfectly true. An endless supply of material things and effort are necessary to maintain the material form. But in time the form must die in spite of the endless supply of material things. But the Self, the Mind, does not die; it never dies. Though a state of attachment can remain even after death, the ego is afraid of death because it is only the ego which can die. That is why the ego-self works continuously to keep the mind attached to the thought that matter is reality and vital if it is not to be destroyed by death. But death is inevitable. The average man lives for three score years and ten, perhaps a little more, then death takes place. The mind survives, life continues, the personal identity is still intact. What then, you may ask, is the purpose of earth life?

Man is **essentially** and **eternally** Spirit which momentarily **uses** matter. The world of matter plays **the** most important role in the development and the progression of the soul. The soul-body is the vital bridge between the state of matter (Body) and Spirit. Here a thousand different questions arise in the mind of the reader the answers to which, at this point, would stagger his imagination and baffle the logical mind. In saying this it must not be assumed that we are beings with the capacity to ask such questions, but are not equipped with the means of finding the answers to them. This would be completely false. Although the **intellect** would find it impossible to answer many of the questions and would be seriously limited in its ability to answer many others, there are existing powers of the higher levels of mind which provide answers on **all** levels. This higher self has the insight and power to convey the Truth, or Reality, of the world which lies beyond our world of senses. The world **beyond** our ego-wall is not so much an intellectual formulation, but a sense of **knowing**, in fact a conviction that the nature of

Absolute Reality, the Eternal State of **Being, is** ourself. In the pursuit of this realisation our short sojourn on earth plays a vital and indispensable part. The intelligences which created the universe and the creatures in it are doubtlessly of infinite variety and of infinite gradation in **development**. Man **must**, therefore, be the **whole** of these varieties commencing with matter and rising through to the infinitely higher levels. If man is commanded to **know himself** then he must eventually come into tune with all levels commencing with the physical. In a later chapter it is hoped to provide sufficient evidence not only of the powers of the higher self, but to prove the indispensable values of the physical world which, together with the intervention of certain spiritual laws, encourages the progression of the soul. But before that it must be realised that eternal man is the **inside** and matter, including the body, is only the outside. Furthermore, that man is not only wrong in believing he is the outside, but it is this very belief that creates all his problems, fears, insecurity and suffering. This very belief **is** the ego-wall.

The ego-wall exists because of man's inexhaustible desire for knowledge and information. The knowledge is usually concerned with the 'things' that go to make up or maintain the ego-wall. This mind can become extremely sophisticated and create a science out of the knowledge. Science means knowledge – knowledge about things, about ways of producing more and more things and in larger quantities. Science tells us about people's desires for things and, later, how to increase the desire. **All** knowledge belongs to the ego, but the ego can never go beyond the wall. It is like asking someone to describe colour. All they can manage is to describe the vehicle. They find it impossible to describe the colour. They cannot go beyond the vehicle. Think of colour as being Absolute Truth and you realise how impossible it is for the intellect to describe it. So it is equally impossible for the ego to recognise, or even be aware of, the **inside**, or inner man. To the ego there is no **inside**. By its own creation, the wall, the ego is totally blind to the inside. The ego mind is fully capable of studying. It has an astonishing capacity for storing knowledge but the knowledge **is** the ego, it belongs only to the ego. Scientists tell us that the brain contains 80–100 million cells. Each cell is capable of storing a complete large library of information. It is possible for the brain to store up every word in the Bible. In fact, every world of every scripture in existence. It can make you an extremely learned man – a genius. But, think about it, all the knowledge will be from the **outside**. It will become just another part of the wall. You will still not understand yourself, God, the Truth, or the Reality, or become enlightened because you will still be on the outside. All the opposite qualities are on the inside. There is, of course, a way in; there is a door because Jesus said, 'Knock and the door shall be opened unto you'. Each man must find the door for himself. Not by a book, a teacher, preacher or guru, but by himself. He must find the **right** way in. The right way is not by knowledge, not even by all the knowledge in the wall. The right way is not via the strength, the tenacity or determination of the ego-mind, nor is it through studying the scriptures, listening to the gurus or a multitude of teachers, or learning **about** philosophy or theology. All these methods simply mean it is the ego knocking on the wall, not on the door, with books, with words of teachers, with systems and methods devised by different schools, with dogmas and creeds. The right way in is only through the state of **being**. The state of **being** is the direct opposite of **knowing about**. The direct opposite of **knowledge**. Knowledge is **knowing about**, knowing everything about the **outside** world, about matter. Man's feelings and emotions are inevitably attached to the outside world of matter, therefore knowledge includes such emotions as jealousy, envy, anger, greed, hate, selfishness, suspicion and possessiveness. All these emotions are an inseparable part of the wall. The materially attached man is he who moves round and round in circles.

It should be of added interest to the reader to note that all action on the physical plane is circular. The circular movement is the natural pattern of all matter. Everything goes round and round, getting nowhere, staying in the same place within the same circular pattern. For instance, the earth moves round the sun. The planets move around each other and the universe.

Atoms move around atoms. The particles and elements comprising the atom, such as electrons and protons, whirl continuously round each other. Water is lifted up from the ocean and deposited as rain once again into the ocean, only to be lifted up again. This is the natural way of all earthly things, but man is not a material thing. He is quite the opposite, but unknowingly strives to adopt a pattern of life in accordance with the way of matter. Man is essentially Spirit. The natural way of Spirit is not by a circular path. It is continuously striving to reach a higher and yet still higher level of consciousness. Man is not naturally a part of the outside world. The sole purpose of his visit to earth is to understand the laws of matter through countless experiences and then, ultimately, to learn that he is not of the physical world. Because man is ignorant of the laws of matter and because he must, for a few years, inhabit a physical body (in the same way that a deep-sea diver must inhabit a diving-suit) he falsely believes he **is** matter. So he tries to organise his life in accordance with physical laws.

Although the physical world is without doubt a world of appearance and phenomena only, and for a time we become its prisoners, we cannot always ignore the reason why it **is** there and why for a limited period only we are its 'prisoners'. The great gods of law know that something of inestimable value must, inevitably, be gained from it and, therefore, it is the business of every soul to know what it is. The achievements on the physical levels are, in themselves, not of great importance. The **real** value of the achievement is to be seen in the **quality** of the character or personality of the doer which emerges. For instance, the intuition, the inspiration, the love, the manifestation of the spiritual qualities which went into the creation, these are the imperishable things. Because we cannot remain indifferent as to why the physical is there, it is every soul's responsibility to find out. Unhappily, the physical experiences which our explorer undertakes to find his natural spiritual way become an addiction. Once a physical achievement has been realised, the results appreciated and, no doubt, enjoyed, other physical plans are conceived and further plans formulated.

Physical action, with its resultant sense of satisfaction, has developed into a habit-forming drug creating a desperate craving for more action. Man becomes 'hooked' on matter. The original goal to find a spiritual pathway, using the world of matter as a base, is gradually but momentarily lost during the efforts of the attainment. The initial stimulus which began with the material now gives way to the determination of the physical mind to preserve the **status quo** and maintain itself in as comfortable a relationship as possible within its physical surroundings. This attitude is eventually reflected in our mental and emotional levels so that we come to accept as normal the things or experiences which create dissatisfaction, stress and anxiety. Nevertheless, we never cease to struggle to improve and add to our immediate environment in the hope of achieving a level which is unchangingly satisfying. This situation is comparable again to the donkey running faster and striving to reach the carrot on the end of the long stick. A man's environment and quality of life are the direct results of the fundamental law of cause and effect. A law which man himself, and no other creature, puts into operation. Most regard this law as only applying to the 'things' of the physical world, but a few, very few, consider it as applying equally to their moral world. And because the mind is not awakened to this fact, man is repeatedly shocked, dismayed and disappointed by the 'things' he took for granted and relied upon for assurance, happiness and stability. Such is the illusionary nature of the outside world. The decision, the plan and the subsequent action taken he may recognise as of his own making, but the disappointing, short-term results and the benefits which quickly disappear will always remain a mystery.

Often, uninvited and seemingly accidentally some great challenge or upheaval plunges unexpectedly into the calm routine of one's life. The mind is naturally disturbed by these sudden aspects of change. Nevertheless, it seems to have innumerable ways of adapting to these altered circumstances. Therefore, no matter how stormy or changeable the situation, some level of the mind will struggle to condition or adapt itself so that once again it attains an **acceptable** level of peace. This process of 'conditioning' or adaptation to changes is constantly operative throughout the physical, emotional, intellectual and spiritual levels of consciousness. Some higher order of mind seems to reach down and touch the lower levels. In this way, through experience after experience, troubled waters are not only momentarity calmed but it is eventually recognised that no matter how uncomfortable these incidents seem to be, we will learn to recognise them as opportunities for spiritual development. It also becomes slowly clear that all spiritual development depends upon the initial stimuli or circumstantial experiences which **produce disharmonies.** These experiences must never be cursed as accidental but, first, as educational periods, then as spiritual opportunities.

These disharmonies are often of great value when potentially obtainable only through the worldly way of action. Some higher laws direct us towards these experiences with the object of bringing about upliftment by systematically eliminating the baser elements of life. The enlightened man willingly accepts that the greatest happiness lies in the acceptance of these difficult elements. Many great teachers accepted this fact and one reminded us of this in a most beautiful prayer. 'Feed me, O Lord, on the bread of tears and give me plenty of tears to drink.' In other words, they knew that wherever inner baser elements were present they would inevitably attract the right actions from the world of appearances. Then the purifying reactions which followed in their wake would bring remorse and, perhaps, demands of renunciation of certain gains and benefits. They saw renunciation not as an action of loss but of expansion. Sages regarded this as the only natural way even though it may be thought by some as the most difficult. Bhakti-yoga also recognises this way of progression. Their prayer says, 'Love, Love the Highest with absolute devotion and all that is ignoble will fall away' – indicating that such a complete love finds God in everything, in suffering, in peace, in ugliness and beauty, in darkness and light.

This way of progression by worldly action (experiences) does not itself lift one up to the spiritual levels of enlightment. First it creates knowledge (often painful) or understanding or the **cause** and the **effect** of the experience. It is much like a person looking at a fire who has never seen or experienced fire at any time. In other words there is a complete state of ignorance concerning this particular phenomenon. Because he is curious and because he has no idea what fire can do, he touches the fire with his hand. The immediate pain and shock which follows instantly transforms the state of ignorance into a state of wisdom. He now knows what fire can do. Never again will he deliberately place his hand on fire. The way of progression is the outworking on a physical level of our baser self. There is no other way. Our choice of action is always the reflection of the desires contained within the lower self. Man has free will to act through greed, envy, jealousy, suspicion, fear or anger. It may even be a desire for power, ambition or fame. On the other hand, he may act through love, compassion or sacrifice. This latter person is free from the entanglements of the ego-wall, the sensual self, the attachment to the things of the world. This man is expressing the consciousness of his spiritual self. The great majority act because of attachment to the 'things' of the world, those temporal things which appeal only to the sensual side of man. They desire only things for themselves. These are the elements which totally blind man to the inner reality which is **himself**.

What distinguishes spirit from matter is that the former is **life** which is continuously active, whilst the latter is passive principle. Spirit evolves and progresses by the life-force which it actually is. Through various experiences, which are provided by exacting laws, the active spirit slowly and eventually disengages itself from the passive matter. The inescapable purpose of life is that spirit shall escape from its embodiment by its **own** efforts and attain individual **self-consciousness** and complete mastery over **all** phases of matter which, because it is temporal, is actually a state of illusion. Before mastery is achieved man's actions are automatic and involuntary responses because they are totally under the influence of the spirit's physical environment. In fact, matter is the womb out of which it must grow and develop by its own life and efforts.

In short, the entire purpose of man's soul during its initial physical stages is the removal of the illusions engendered by its imprisonment in time, space and matter. The spirit or soul achieves freedom only when it understands fully the nature of the ego-wall (matter and its emotional attachments to it) and returns to the Centre – Reality. Time, space and matter are essential to the life of the ego. The ego **is** the wall and the wall can only remain conscious of itself and for this reason the ego finds it impossible to penetrate to the Centre. To achieve mastery over matter man must become enlightened which means he must develop **knowledge** concerning the true nature of matter.

Enlightenment is only achieved by the spirit's struggle against the temptations and demands of the ego-mind. Intellectual study of theology, creeds and dogmas will not help. Information from the Bible, the Koran, the Bhagavad Gita or Vedas will not help. All this is nothing but information being gathered in by the wall. It is nothing but words. Information comes only from the **outside**.

What is enlightenment? It is simply becoming aware of yourself. Enlightenment means turning your back on the wall and going towards the source, and the sources are to be found only in one place – **within yourself**! Why ask someone else or search through many books when you are searching for something you already have? All mystics claim to have had an experience which, in its deeper form, is incommunicable in words. How then can it be got from a book or a teacher. Many think about the mystics and their experiences of Reality and believe they have a gift which few people have. That is man's greatest illusion. There are no insurmountable fences between man's lowest levels of consciousness and his absolute spiritual levels. In truth, there are no levels on which mystical experiences are not possible. Every level, even the humblest, is a vital expression of the divine being. Enlightened ones are aware that **some** aspect of the highest self acts and constantly lives through the lower levels which we call the ego. This must be so because the great Hindu classic, the Bhagavad Gita, tells us, 'All action [meaning life] originates in the Supreme Spirit which is imperishable and in all sacrificial action the all-pervading Supreme Spirit is constantly present.' It must, therefore, be realised that there never can be **full** enlightenment unless it is experienced and retained on *every* level of consciousness.

A great prophet was once heard to say that an enlightened man lives exactly the way of an ordinary man. He eats when he feels hungry. Drinks when he is thirsty. Sleeps when he feels tired. He laughs and smiles at the very same things. There are no differences on the **outside**. The enlightened man looks **at** the outside world but he is not **in** it; he is not a part of it. He looks outside but he remains inside. Of course, he uses the things of the world for the body's essential maintenance, necessary shelter and basic comforts, but he is not **attached** to them. The ego-wall cannot exist for him, whereas the unenlightened man spends all his time looking outwards to life. He sees only the things which are there – that have **always** been there, but he is completely ignorant regarding the power that created them. Therefore he is blind and deaf to the All-Power, which means there is a part of the unenlightened man which is completely dead. This man's world is simply a vast collection of 'things', but he, at this stage of his progression, has only the capacity to respond to them with a collection of feelings. These feelings are experienced through the mind as recognition of those things which the mind enjoys in a sensual way and, therefore, frequently demands. The mind creates the habit of thinking about the objects of pleasure distributed throughout the world. The next step which develops is that the mind becomes totally obsessed with the sense world which now appears as the only reality. The mind has reached the ultimate ignorance, the densest of the blinding veils which ultimately leads us to the belief that we are only the ego. Nevertheless, the quest for happiness continues to lure man on. The cravings and desires become greater and more frustrating but the mind continually fails to realise that these are only the futile efforts of the ego-mind's search for happiness and security. The real self, which is eternal and infinite, has no need to attain anything, not even happiness, because it is the realisation of **everything**. The ego is closely encompassed by its own thoughts. The walls are very familiar to it. They are its world, its home. It has been living in it for so long it has become blissfully accustomed to it. It is the only real thing it has. The self has become a prisoner, and like all prisoners who have been in prison too long, it is afraid to come out. It is afraid of freedom. Freedom means death to the wall, to all things it has treasured and which have helped to create it. Ironically, on the other side of the wall there waits the infinite, eternal you which strives for nothing and desires nothing because it is the **whole self** – the whole of everything. But to the ego-mind the infinite appears like death. It has become accustomed to the solid, finite, clear-cut boundaries in spite of the struggles, efforts and frustrations they present. When man is freed from the obstructing wall and lives from the Centre, life is infinitely different. There no one dies, nothing **can** die, death is impossible, an illusion. But for those who live on the outside of the wall, everyone dies. Death happens all the time. They have killed the soul and preserved the body. The enlightened person has killed the body and developed the soul.

All problems, fears and sufferings arise because the ego-wall is fragmented. It is forever striking outwards in every direction towards all finite things. This is disunity, chaos and disharmony. Mind can only understand those things which can be analysed, touched, seen, tasted, heard and smelt. These are the divided, fragmented parts of matter; the temporal trouble-spots of matter. They are the things which are constantly dying and must be replaced over and over again. To the earthly mind the process never stops; it doesn't expect or want it to stop.

Therefore, as long as the ego-mind is in command, man will continue to move round and round the wall finding it impossible to reach the Centre. Man can learn about matter by making a study of it but in this way he will never know about the inner-consciousness, because matter, and all knowledge concerning it, remains on the outside. Matter has no Centre. Many students of theology and other orders attempt to reach the Centre by collecting knowledge. All knowledge and information which are collected and stored belong to the brain. The brain is the lighthouse of the wall. It searches, finds and stores all the information in one of its millions of library-cells. The ego-mind can be an excellent, first-class student. It can memorise perfectly every word in the Bible, in every scripture throughout the world. It can make you a religious genius, but you will still remain totally ignorant of the presence of the inner-consciousness – the Centre, because all this information is of the outside. You many know all **about** the scriptures, but the problem is you have not **become** them. To claim that you know all **about** truth, scriptures or God means you know absolutely nothing. **All** truth comes only from the Centre. The Divine-God, the All-Truth **is** the Centre, so how can the ego, which is totally unaware of the existence of the Centre, claim to know about God or Truth? How can you who are constantly walking round and round the wall claim to know about God when the way to God is on a straight line **from** the wall to the Centre.

A great spiritual teacher said, 'knock and the door shall be opened unto you.' The problem is that those who seek God start knocking on the wall with a book; with words borrowed from a teacher; with information. Again they are starting from the outside. They hope to find the door through information, like treasure hunters using a map or a compass. The secret of the way to the door lies in a simple truth: **become** the Jesus, **become** the Buddha, **become** the Krishna, **become** the scriptures. Don't waste time **knowing** about the Masters of Truth. When you realise this you will find that the door has always been there, has always been open. Don't learn **about** others who know the truth. Before you can know truth you must turn your back on the wall, only then will you be enlightened. What is enlightenment? It is simply becoming aware of the nature of the wall, knowing you are not a part of it. Only then will you become aware of your true self, your spiritual self. Then you are enlightened. This revelation only takes place when you become totally unaware of the outside world; when you forget all about information, about the Bible, about the Gita, the Koran and the gurus. They are all part of the wall. These outside agents cannot tell you about **your** inner world. You are already there, you are already **it**. Do not remain a seeker; become the enlightened. As long as you remain a seeker you remain unenlightened.

Inside every man there is the cry within the heart for the truth, the hunger of the soul for freedom. The one question which remains is: which way to go, in what direction? The search for freedom, for truth, is much like climbers scaling a difficult mountain. There are so many pathways. Some decide to take one pathway and others take another. As long as all keep climbing they will all meet on the summit where all paths converge.

I hope that the interpretation I have made of the inner-reality has given the reader some idea of the goal and he is now concerned only with the way to it. I have written about the principal barrier, the ego-wall, which is only a collection of things and feelings of attachment which go together to create the wall. The lower mind of man is simply a collection of emotions, feelings and information. And when the things of the outer world and the lower mind are drawn together, we get what Buddha describes as **attachment**. 'In attachment' he says, 'see suffering.' The practical problem facing the awakening soul is the dissolving of the wall, the detachment of the mind from the desire for the illusionary sensual things of the outer world. When the mystics and masters referred to this world as the illusionary world, they were referring only to the experiences for which we crave and live by, the experiences in which we seek pleasure without the realisation that they last but a few moments and then fade into absolute nothingness. The mind demands sensual experiences and this can only be taken from the things of the world. A bar of chocolate, a beefburger, a new suit of clothes, a sleek motor car afford a feeling of excitement to the senses. But the experiences quickly die leaving behind only a memory of the sensual experience. Once established, this memory-cell, from time to time, reminds the sensual mind of the experience and demands that it be repeated again and again. When each singular experience dies, this is the **total** death, the only death which man undergoes. Like the knowledge and the information previously collected they were created only to die. The sensory things are the only dead things in life. Total, sustained satisfaction cannot be provided by objects that die an instantaneous death. Your Being, the inner-consciousness **is** life, the only **undying** life. It cannot die, it is Reality, therefore the momentary experience, its opposite, must be illusion.

What, therefore, must the ego-mind do to bring about its own death and disappearance and so leave the Supreme-Self in full possession? In spite of all I have said about the temporal ego-mind and its constant attraction to the finite, sensory things of the world and about the inner-consciousness, which is the ultimate goal of all men, there must be some reason for the inclusion of this disturbing, temporal phase in man's existence. There must be some gain to the Supreme-Self. The most important fact to remember is that a part, or some aspect, of the Supreme-Self is immersed in, and lives through, the ego's life. Therefore, we must assume that all seekings, strivings and the aspiring of the ego-self must really be expressions of the immersed Supreme-Self's promptings. As we have observed from our travels in life, there are many souls who are totally unsuited, temperamentally and spiritually, to go along a particular road to enlightenment. If the Supreme-Self prompting **each** ego-being it is, obviously, in its great wisdom, urging it along a particular road (which could be fraught with frustration, illusion and pain) which will **ultimately**, and surely, bring it to the desired goal.

The tragedy of most narrow-minded sectarian schools, who have experienced no mystical insight or received no intuitive wisdom, is that they believe there is only one way for every soul, irrespective of its spiritual ability and insight. They suppose, because of their great literal knowledge and their extensive absorbtion of the scriptures, that they are standing on the peaks of Truth, whereas, in truth, they are standing on molehills.

However, whatever the gains achieved by the higher-self by its temporal absorbtion into the lower levels of consciousness, I shall consider these in the next chapter.

CHAPTER THREE

THE NATURE OF THE WORLD

Ever since man has been conscious of himself he has been searching for something. Something which he knows, instinctively, lies not on the outside. Without doubt he is searching for happiness, some kind of peace and security in a world in which, apart from wars, turmoil and environmental strife, he senses an inner disquiet, dissatisfaction and unfulfilment. He seeks by going from one leader to another, from one religious organisation to another, from one job to another.

Though he is seeking happiness, it is **satisfaction** that he all too often finds. but is that what he is really seeking? Does he mistake it for happiness? Is he aware that there is a great difference between happiness and satisfaction? Is it possible to **search** for happiness? No doubt he can find satisfaction in many things, but can he really find happiness? Surely, happiness, when we think about it, is really derivative; it is the **after-effect** of something else. Happiness can be likened to the phenomenon of love. We cannot see or experience love by itself, it must have an object. Therefore, happiness is the after-effect, or by-product, of some other activity. So before we can continue with our search, we must give considerable thought, and earnest attention to decide what it is we want – happiness or satisfaction. Unfortunately, most people are expecting some kind of reward and satisfaction. After all their labours and efforts they want to achieve a sense of fullness and satisfaction.

After years of effort and repeated experiences of the sense of satisfaction, we discover that we are still seeking for something permanent, some way to succeed in becoming successful in a particular enterprise. Men develop a feeling of fulfilment and satisfaction, but, whether they realise it or not, they are still seeking. Satisfaction they have realised, but not happiness. They have not solved the real problem.

To achieve total isolation in a self-made world of success, satisfaction and achievement will never lead to total release from the deeper levels of unrest. So, first, we must find out what it is that each of us is seeking **inwardly** and **outwardly** and needing so much. Once this realisation is understood and achieved we will then know that it is not necessary to go anywhere, to any teacher, church organisation or library. The one big difficulty is being absolutely sure within ourselves concerning **what** we wish to find and **how** we go about finding it. These are the biggest problems. How **can** we be sure and does that assurance come through searching outwardly, through trying to find out what others are saying? Can we get it from the best and most exalted teachers in the land or from the local preacher?

In our haste, impatience and sincere desire to find out, we talk to every promising person, read innumerable books, attend many meetings and seminars – trying to find answers to our outer and inner conflicts, to the miseries and frustrations in our life. Throughout all these activities and multifarious 'wisdoms' given out by the many well-meaning teachers and religious organisations, we find nothing permanent, nothing lasting. That something which the wise call Truth, God, the Infinite continues to evade us. It seems that all we have collected so far is a lot of information, facts and methods. Information which simply tells us what other people believe, are doing and thinking, but which we have failed to know **within** ourselves. We have not had the **direct experience**. We have not experienced that which is known as the **permanent**. In all truth we have not yet found out what it is we are seeking – that something which will give us a sense of **permanency**; permanent satisfaction, permanent happiness and the permanent sense of **being** even when we have stripped ourselves of all the words, the teachings, the methods, the books and even the sense of searching. Only then will we **know** the reality which is Truth, which is God – which is **ourself**.

So we come to the most vital point where we must ask ourselves earnestly and profoundly if Truth and permanent happiness can be given to us by someone else whilst we remain ignorant of our real self? Surely, the reader must realise that as long as he has no understanding of himself there is no basis for the right kind of thought. Where does the search begin? As long as he remains ignorant of himself, remains unaware of the **whole** man, there cannot be a basis for a beginning of the search for **self**. Without this basis the thoughts will continue to go out in the wrong direction, away from the Truth, from the Reality. Before we can prepare the right basis, we must first think about a transformation of ourselves. But before we can transform, we must know exactly who we are and what we are. If we are petty, jealous, vain, greedy, selfish, suspicious and ambitious, that is the society **we** have created and the society we live in. That is positive attachment to materialism – to the outer self. Such a situation prompted Buddha to say, 'In attachment see suffering'. Buddha also taught that to live in such a society is to experience three conditions: 'change and impermanence, the unreality of the ego-self, and suffering'.

What is it we call permanent? What is the real nature of that which we are seeking. Are we seeking permanent happiness, permanent satisfaction, permanent security or permanent love? Therefore, surely, we must fully understand the thing we are searching for. All of our life we have experimented with various actions, in the hope that they will bring us permanent satisfaction or happiness, but in every case they have eventually faded away and, sadly we have found ourselves back in square one. So, again, I must remind the reader that he must fully understand the thing he is seeking and what, he hopes will give him permanent satisfaction. The searcher must fully understand himself. Why is he unhappy, why does complete satisfaction continue to evade him? Perhaps the kind of permanency he is seeking does not exist. Now Truth is something entirely different. In fact, Truth **is** entirely different to that which you can touch, see, hear, taste and smell. Is it on these lines that the seeker is seeking permanency? Therefore, before he can find permanent happiness or satisfaction, the seeker must understand the thing he is seeking, why he is seeking and with which level of mind he is seeking because, to the ego-mind, or earth-mind, there is no such thing as permanent happiness, security or truth. Therefore, so long as we remain ignorant of our selves, so long as we remain unaware of the **Whole-Self** there is no basis for correct thought, to receive the right guidance, to begin our search. Without recognising your own particular way of thinking, why you believe in certain things, why you hold on to certain beliefs, such as religion or social politics, why you think in a certain way about your neighbours and friends, without recognising the **True Substance** and quality of your thoughts and, in addition, from which level of consciousness they originate, your search will be futile and all action will be without benefit.

Before we can begin to understand the purpose of life, the purpose of pain, fear and insecurity, why there are wars and conflicts within ourselves and the community **we must begin with ourselves**. That is, the **Whole-Self**. This is far from being an easy course of action. In fact, it is extremely difficult to search for oneself. To recognise how our thoughts operate, to recognise the quality of our thoughts, we have to be extraordinarily alert, so that we become more and more aware not only of the complexities of our thoughts, but also of the quality of our responses to certain experiences and towards others. Jesus commanded his disciples to stay awake. By this he meant they had to be constantly aware of the quality of their thoughts, actions and reactions. He also said that even by your thoughts you can injure others, but not as much as you hurt yourself. Only in this way is it possible to develop a greater awareness not only of oneself, but also of others with whom we are in constant contact. When Krishna said we must pray continuously, he did not mean we have to be on our knees all day, but to be always conscious of the spiritual quality of our thoughts and actions – or the lack of it.

To know oneself is to study oneself in action whilst in relationship with others, responding to different circumstances, different experiences and different people. The greatest difficulties arise because we have already committed ourselves to numerous and varied activities, such as earning a living, organising the household, caring for a family, raising children, or have taken on the responsibilities of certain organisations. We have committed ourselves in so many different ways that we have little time for self-reflection; to observe others; to study ourselves. Sensitive people develop a manner of impatience and sometimes irritation because they are anxious to get on. They want to achieve an end; to feel something. They sense that they should be doing something much more important, something more fulfilling. So they have little opportunity for self-observation. The frustration continues and builds up. Such people, in order to overcome this frustration, try to seek a more convenient way by pursuing gurus and teachers and by the reading of their books, their methods and ideas. This is not the right way because the responsibility of knowing oneself rests entirely with oneself. It is good to listen to experienced and enlightened philosophers, but do not absorb without question. If he speaks truth it will never die within you. That which is truth will reveal itself in your life as you act and relate to others. On the other hand you may seek audience with a thousand gurus, teachers and their particular systems, you may travel from one end of the earth to the other, but always in the end you will have to come back to yourself. Coming back to ourselves, recognising ourselves **is the truth**. As most of us are totally unaware of the true nature of ourselves it can be very difficult to recognise what we are looking for.

Self-knowledge does not offer us a final solution to our search. There is no final solution. There can never be total achievement because achievement means we have come to a conclusion. We are in search of the **Whole-Self** and the Whole-Self is not to be compared with a complete bar of chocolate or a beefburger. There is a definite end to these things. Once the experience has been extracted, it is no more, its life is finished. The Whole-Self is an endless river. As we continue to study the self, as we learn more and more, we achieve a greater understanding, a deeper understanding which comes from within. Without this understanding, without this self-experience it is futile to read books or listen to teachers. Whereas when one is beginning to **know**, this is a development of the understanding of the Whole-Self. There is created something that is not of the everyday mind. There takes place a subtle and unusual transformation of the immediate relationship between you, the people, and the immediate world in which you live. This is the beginning of an inner tranquillity which expresses a **creative** happiness. Study the faces of spiritual teachers, gurus and mystics and you not only see the gentleness, but you feel it. These are the people who have first studied the self, recognised the accumulated mind and so have come to understand the Whole-Self. The Whole-Self is love and wisdom.

Enlightenment means Self-Knowledge, Total-Knowledge or Self-Awareness. Enlightenment is not a slow process as is the process of studying mathematics, languages or business management. It will be immediate. Of course, the preparation will be long and often frustrating. You will experience much impatience and many times the intruding mind will suggest that you are wasting your time, but the actual experience of enlightenment will be rapid like a sudden leap from the floor of a valley to a mountain top. My experience of enlightenment was exactly like that. One moment I was sad, spiritually low and feeling somewhat desolate, then, in a moment, there was this sudden flash of enlightenment. The deep inner knowing of the self, of life, has never ceased to be. During meditation, understanding of various problems of life immediately flood the consciousness. Remember that all gradual processes belong solely to the logical or earthly mind but enlightenment lies far beyond that mind which is totally incapable of understanding it. Mind is capable of understanding parts of man but the Whole-Man will always elude it. So if you are relying on mind which is always to be found in the market place of worldly things you will never succeed in reaching the deep Inner-Self. Mind is capable of being a great scholar. It can be a great teacher – a genius of worldly things. It can **study** enlightenment, it can study scripture and books about God, it can even pretend to know everything about enlightenment, about religion and about God, but enlightenment is not something you can understand – there can only be the **Direct Experience** of the Whole-Self. To **know** anything or everything about the Whole-Self means you know nothing about the reality of the Whole-Self. Knowledge, any amount of knowledge, is not the Direct-Experience, is not the Truth. You can know everything about matter and all the things it can create, but you cannot know about consciousness. Consciousness is the unknown. Everything you know, including the body and brain is of the outside. The Whole-Self, including the highest levels of consciousness, is the vital centre of man. Modern science has advanced to incredible depths but it is still simply knowledge. Knowledge about every aspect of the outside; in fact, every place where there is no Centre. Words, books, facts, information and knowledge are the results of science, but you cannot approach the Centre through science – you have **to become it**! You cannot know about Truth, you must **become** Truth. You cannot know about Enlightenment you must **become** it. In other words the state of **being** is awareness **there.**

There is not need to go to anyone because you will always come back to the same point – **yourself**! You may read the works of masters and mystics, you may even wish you could go to a master, but all he can do is give you instructions or guidance, which is knowledge, on how you can reach **yourself**. No master, or mystic or sage can give you the direct experience. They can only tell you to look within yourself. Man spends a lot of time looking, examining, collecting knowledge of that which is already there, which has always been there. But he spends no time at all thinking about the power that created it and put it there. Science, in spite of its phenomenal advances and its collection of highly sophisticated instruments, cannot go beyond the things that have always been there. Science is incapable of creating anything new. It discovers nothing that is new. The knowledge it uncovers is old. How can something be new when it has always been there? Scientists simply uncover it. The mind, like science, is old. It simply collects knowledge about things that have always been there. Mind and science go together, they are inseparable. They are only capable of collecting information about things of the sense world. Mind cannot conceive anything new because it is only capable of repeating things with the help of the memory, the things that have always been known and always been there. The mind is totally incapable of creating the original. The **new**, the **original** will only be found in the deep inner-consciousness, never in the mind.

Bring this thought constantly to your consciousness – you are **already** the Absolute Reality, you are **already** the Absolute Freedom, the Absolute Wisdom, Truth and Love. They have always been there within you, the **real, original** you has always **been**. Unfortunately, the realisation is not there because positioned between you and the realisation is the mind, a solid wall of things which include sensory objects, desires, ambitions, books, printed scriptures, words of teachers, etc. You are like a man standing inches away, facing a brick wall. You are becoming more and more angry, frustrated and frightened because you are unable to go forward, not realising that you are facing the wrong way. The way to freedom lies behind you.

All that is new and original is born out of the Inner Consciousness. The journey you are about to take is a new, original journey. The mind is simply a collection of innumerable old journeys, futile journeys which have led to nowhere, but merely added to the endless collection of useless memories. Revolutions are always created by attempts to destroy old ideas, methods, thoughts and habits. That is why no revolution in existence is more necessary to the soul than **mind-revolution**. However, no revolution is possible without meditation. All methods of meditation are nothing more than ways to revolutionise the mind so that the innermost consciousness eventually rises to the surface and the old mind is pushed to one side, eventually to be forgotten. The new mind reflects its reality. Everything becomes new, life takes on a new dimension. A whole new truth is revealed in everything which before you took for granted. Life ceases to be full of fears and anxieties. You realise that death has never occurred in the world at any time – **life is eternal.**

CHAPTER FOUR

THE NATURE OF MAN

It has already been stressed in previous chapters that before we can set out on the long journey to find Reality and Truth, before we can find out what the essential end-purpose of this life is, it is essential that we begin to understand ourselves first. That is, we must begin to understand the **total nature** of man - the **Whole-Man.** But to know oneself is to study oneself in action - mental and physical. That entails studying every aspect of **all** actions in **all** circumstances. This must necessarily include all relationships with others in our society.

What is the relationship between man and the miseries, confusions and the various conflicts in society which he fears? These disturbances could not possibly come into being by themselves. People create them during their relationships with each other. In truth, what they are **within** themselves they have projected outwardly to the rest of the community. That which lies deep within are their feelings, thoughts, desires, ambitions and jealousies. All these things are continuously projected outwardly. These projections are all that constitutes not only our family relationships, the immediate community, our environment, but our world. If we project love, understanding, compassion and tolerance that also becomes not only our society, but also our world. If our projections are selfishness, impatience, arrogance and greed then that becomes the quality of our society and world. In other words, what **you are** the world becomes. Your projections become society's projections. What of the source of these projections? Do we want to bring about certain alterations from the motive of benefiting society, the family, the world or just ourselves? Remember that the present society was created by an individual or community of people who had similar ideas. An unhappy society, or family, is based upon the discontent and confusion of those who are concerned about the way they live or by the way they **want** to live. Naturally, everyone is concerned with their daily existence. Discontent, confusion, insecurity and all the lower-level emotions such as greed, envy, jealousy and fear are created by situations dealing with jobs, earning money, relationships with the family or neighbours, lust for power, beliefs and desires: this is the creative fabric of a self-constructed society. This kind of society, or community, is constructed by thoughts, and, if we are truly honest about it, is based on egocentricity. Instead of concentrating on earning a living and achieving a reasonable standard of security, many strive to achieve a situation superior to that of their neighbours'. Once having achieved a little more they become consumed by the desire to acquire more and more, not caring very much how the neighbours are managing. Most people want prestige, position and power because the truth is that most people are egocentric. Egocentricity is one of the destructive factors in a society because it reflects a desire for power and authority which in turn creates a power-politics complex.

Man needs the relationship of a society but must discover the real relationship. What is the relationship based upon? If most people are concerned about improving their social status or adding to their financial security it cannot, therefore, be based upon love of humanity. If it was based upon love of community, upon love of one another, there would develop an unchanging happiness, peace and a high standard of social order and harmony. On the other hand let us imagine that every person in the community is of equal thought, equal love and respect. Would it not be true that there would be no ill-will, no individuals with the desire to dominate which would arouse jealousy, passion and anger? There would be no avenues for initiative, no ambition, which means there would be no disciples or teachers, no leaders or inspirers. What would happen to our natural self-protective instinct or individualised ideas? What about the religious, the not-so-religious and the unbelievers? Would not the community be geared down to the slowest unimaginative individual? Therefore, when we live in any society, be it religious or not, a business base or a community farm, the natural and differing concepts of the inhabitants will, at some time, automatically come into conflict and sooner or later separate man from man in family and nationalism. So the very big problem is whether we can live in a society which is static. Though it may seem idealistic, the truth is that no society could survive once it ceases to be progressive. For such a society to succeed it must, ironically, create a revolution within each individual. There are battles going on in countries all over the world, hopefully designed to bring about social reform and so-called freedom through communistic policies and other methods, but in every instance the action is undertaken with total regard for the **outer** structures, position and possessions of man. However sincere and radical that social revolution may be, by its very nature the achievements, if any, are doomed to fail, and the benefits bound to be short-lived or sporadic because they give no thought to the **inward** revolution of the individual necessary to bring about a psychological transformation. Therefore, to create a society which is not robotic, not static or simply living on 'hand-outs', it is vital for the individual to achieve a transformation concerning his ideals, thoughts, ambitions and general direction of his way of progression. Without this **inward** psychological revolution, to put effort only into the transformation of the outer circumstances has virtually no significance at all. What is symbolic of a static society, no matter how wisely legislation may be advanced, is that the community will always be in a state of decay and want because progress and revolution must always start from **within** and not merely outwardly.

Outward action no matter how repeatedly or perfectly it is accomplished always, in time, comes to an end simply because the outside world is static. Preoccupation with the outside actions of a society, because of the constant need for creation and re-creation, totally absorbs the individual, therefore making him equally static and robotic. This punishing, demanding and chaotic state will prevail until the individual realises that constant, creative revolution can only begin within himself, not in society and never in the outer world. Constantly we are witness to societies crumbling and disintegrating, so we continue to look more and more to architects, designers, builders, politicians and religious counsellors. But again and again society continues to deteriorate to the same conditions as before. To understand that which is crumbling and why we continue to fail and to prevent the deterioration, we must examine the outside structure carefully within ourselves. We must stop depending upon the architects without and start looking to the architects within. In other words we must positively investigate and recognise the real nature of the world outside, because the problems which create the deterioration of the outer body are the same problems which affect the outer world. Every country in the world is a population of imitators. We copy everything outwardly, that is everything that already exists and has always existed. We do not know how to be inwardly creative. We copy the techniques of others when communicating with each other, we copy the words of teachers and preachers. Practically the whole of our educational system, social behaviour and religious beliefs are all based upon imitation. We have ceased to be our genuine selves. Ours is a robotic society because every time we rely upon conditional responses. All over the world there are 'patterned' societies and religions, each equipped with repetitive responses specially conditioned according to whether the individual is Catholic, Protestant, Hindu, Buddhist, Taoist, Scottish, English, German or French. All responses are conditioned according to the nature of specific parts of the world and the pattern of its society. The problems of the individual are so colossal and so complex that for him to understand them and to resolve them, he must realise that the problems of the world are equally complex and colossal even though they are the same problems. All are **seemingly** of the outside. In truth there are no problems in the outside world they are only within man himself.

Though it is necessary for man to travel through the world, it is not necessary for him to be part of it. The outside, a sense world, is a world of millions of people each with their own particular problems, fears, emotions and desires, all different and personal. Man has no control whatsoever over this outside world but, always, he has complete control over his inside world and it is only when he loses control over this inner world, when he throws out his own fears, anxieties, emotions and desires, that a confict is created. The world is simply a collection of sensual things, and man is essentially a collection of feelings. Problems and disharmonies arise when the feelings of man and the things of the world become attached to each other. As Buddha said, 'In attachment see suffering.' When man becomes attached to the world of sense, he experiences three conditions: 1. constant change; 2. the unreality of the ego (material) mind, 3. suffering. The senses of man, sight, hearing, smell, touch and taste, thirst for the sensual experiences to be extracted from the things of the world. But bring to mind the thought that the life of the 'thing' lasts only as long as experience is forthcoming. Then the thing, the object, is no more. It is, in truth, as an illusion, but the demand of the senses for the sensual experience to be repeated again and again calls for continuous daily effort. The non-stop demands bring pressure to bear upon our resources and upon our ability to maintain the supply. The result is that two basic fears are manifested. One is the fear that our resources may not always be sufficient, but if this is not so, then the other fear is the prevalent thought of the possibility of losing those things and resources we already possess.

The solution to these everyday fears lies not in the short supply or abundance of the things we consider essential to our contentment and well-being, or the difficulties and efforts encountered to ensure the supply, but in the creator of the problems which is ourselves. Unless we understand the nature of the world, that is, the things it tempts us with and the nature of that aspect of ourselves which is subject to temptation, it will be very difficult to escape from the grip of the sensual mind. The things of the world and the momentary experiences the sensual mind extracts from them are not real, not substantial. Always in the end you are left with nothing but a memory of the sensual experience. They are the stuff dreams are made of. They are short-lived ripples in the mind. And the meaning? There is no meaning whatsoever. And the purpose? There is no purpose, just a quick flash of pleasure then there is nothing left. All that worry and the effort of getting the things still remains with us because there is no satisfaction, no lasting accomplishment. So we are compelled to move on, going round and round like the mouse in the revolving wheel. Nevertheless, the world is not something we must strive to separate ourselves from. The world, its societies and the relationships we establish are the things we need. The world itself is not the problem nor are the things which appear so tempting. The problem, I repeat, is ourselves. To attempt to withdraw from the world of things is not a solution because we cannot live in isolation. To reach the truth is to be related, but with an understanding of the **nature** of the place we live in and the nature of ourselves. Whilst there cannot be such a thing as living in isolation, it is the absence of the **right relationship** that brings misery, fear and conflicts involving envy, jealousy, greed, suspicion and selfishness. World involvement, or relationship, is important only when we can achieve a transformation - a revolution - then we begin, actively, to achieve the **right relationship** with the outside world. Real inner revolution is not according to a particular method, pattern, scripture or teacher. It is a revolution of **values**, a revolution from **sensual** values to values which are not temporal experiences created by environmental attractions or influences. To find these true values which will bring about a radical transformation, or regeneration, it is vitally essential to begin with ourselves. All the world's problems, our problems, are within ourselves. Self-knowledge is the beginning of truth, the first step on the pathway to the inner-self.

To know oneself there must be the will to accept **everything** about ourself. That is where the biggest problem lies. Naturally, everyone wants to be transformed because almost everybody is discontented, afraid and insecure. Discontent and seeming injustices cause us to question the purpose of life, the existence of God, the standards of other people. Discontent may, for a time, set us aflame determined to overcome the causes of our discontent, but because we have canalised our discontent (using the same motives and methods in the hope of achieving better results) we eventually give up hope and lose the drive to overcome. That is why it is vital that we start by discovering ourselves. Self-knowledge cannot possibly be given to us through a book, scriptures, or the words of a friend or teacher. Without knowing what you are, the true nature of your motives, and which aspect of yourself is doing the searching, there is no basis for a correct search.

The problem is getting to know oneself as one **really** is, not as one wishes to be which is nothing more than a dream. It is fictitous, unreal and ambitious. Remember, it is only that part of you which **is**, the unsavoury part that can be transformed, not that which you want to be – that is unreal. Never, never create an image of what you want to be. That is ambition. Never try to follow a method or prepare a pattern of behaviour because this is limitation and restriction. If you really want to know who you really are, or what you are, then you cannot create a pattern of what you are not. Always there must be an alertness of mind, there must always be the courage to face, recognise and accept the things about you which are not good. Sit quietly and contemplate the actions and behaviour you know. To recognise that you are greedy, egotistical, violent, lustful, selfish, suspicious, jealous, envious, proud, joyful of authority or spiteful requires an extraordinary perception. It requires honesty, courage and clarity of thought. Where alertness is needed is to detect when the outer mind is making excuses for all that is ugly.

The acceptance of what you are, whether it be bad, evil, dishonest, good or beautiful, is the beginning of the transformation. The faculty of virtue is beginning to develop. Virtue is vital for correct spiritual guidance. It awakens the conscience which is quick to recognise incorrect attitudes and bad behaviour. Virtue recognises truth and will immediately send out a warning via a sense of remorse should truth be misused or ignored. If we wish to understand someone who is not moral, virtue allows us to observe and study him without condemning him. To condemn anyone is to display ignorance of his ideas, motives and the reasons why he is acting that way. Virtue allows us to realise that **everyone** is the son of God. That aspect we must learn to recognise and understand is an inescapable part of every living thing. Observe the movements of other people, the use of words, idiosyncrasies, expressions, their feelings. To condemn a person means there is no comprehension of **any** aspect of that person.

The fundamental revolution within oneself does not come directly from knowledge or from notes gathered from various experiences; this is merely the culmination of memory. Self-knowledge is a gradual, subtle development. If we decide to collect knowledge, we are merely developing a system or method which eventually becomes a static centre which seriously limits the development of a deeper understanding. To understand what **is**, what we really **are**, requires a state of mind in which there is no **identification** of specific items within and no condemnation of what we observe in others, only a justifiable condemnation of ourselves. When there is a strong, genuine desire to understand ourselves, when there develops an intensity of interest, the right state of mind develops.

Preachers, teachers, good Samaritans and even philosophers can easily design a system or method for you, but remember, any and every system is always a fixed pattern. Systems have a specific beginning, therefore they must have a predictable result which would be confined to the pattern. If I were to follow a particular, prepared method or pattern designed to know myself, then the results must necessarily be limited to the outline of the method which means I will only **partly** know myself. This would follow because I would be confining my thinking, my actions and reactions strictly to the method. Even if I follow the method exactly and faithfully it would not necessarily result in an understanding of myself, it would simply prove that I am capable of faithfully following a pattern. Many good and sincere people unwittingly follow a pattern. They go regularly to church and study the Bible, the Koran, the Talmud, the Bhagavad Gita and so on. They are given a prepared prayer and sermon to memorise and think about. These people are within the confines, the pattern, or prison of the scriptures. And once in the grip of the scriptures – the words – it is extremely difficult to gain freedom. The words become static prisons. Words are just items of knowledge to fill the brain cells. Many people feel that they must go to church because there is nowhere else to go. The church is filled with statues, books of scripture and symbols to which they pray. This reminds me of a true story of a famous Buddhist monk. One morning he was found sitting by the roadside putting flowers around a milestone. He began to worship the milestone and pray to it. Another passing monk stopped and remarked, 'You fool, what are you doing? This is not a statue of Buddha.' The first monk replied, 'When you have the feeling to pray, everything is a statue of Buddha.' Which proves the point that there is no **method** to achieve self-realisation. All methods belong to the outside. The approach to self-realisation is very much the same as applying spiritual healing. During my trips around the world I have witnessed many peculiar and bizarre healing techniques. There was the healer who 'blew' the healing power via a trumpet into the patient. Another who placed plastic dolls over the affected part of the body and then prayed that the disease would enter into the doll and so relieve the sick person. Yet another who ran around the room then leapt high in the air, pulled down the healing power from the air and thrust it through the patient. Just as strange was the healer who 'combed' every part of the patient's body in order to pull out the disharmonious influences. Others specialised in mending cracks and holes in 'damaged' auras to prevent the vital energy from flowing from the sick person's body. These techniques may seem very humorous, weird and fanatical but the amazing thing is that most of these sick people actually received a great deal of benefit and often many were completely cured. The cure or the benefits were not caused by the different techniques, but by the healer's sincere and honest desire to help these people. The sincerity had a spiritual motive; it was compassion. Spiritual motives and compassion are pure expressions of the soul **within**. Therefore, the healing came from **within** and not from the physically demonstrated techniques. In the same way, there is no technique to achieve self-realisation.

Life itself, everything and every soul in it, is divine. Wherever there is love, sincerity and compassion, everywhere you sit, or stand, becomes a cathedral. If we follow systems and methods we must have instructors, guides, authorities, gurus and saviours who are **expected** to guarantee everything we desire. That cannot possibly be the right way to self-realisation. The greatest teachers can always describe the way ahead but they cannot walk the pathway for you. It is always true that under the sheltering belief of a guide, teacher, guru or master we may adopt a temporal sense of security, a sense of things going well, but that will never amount to the **total** understanding of oneself. This kind of guidance, by its very nature, bars the way to complete self-awareness because there must always be total freedom of the self. Total freedom is the very essence of self-realisation.

Self-realisation is not something that can be learned from others. Like Truth it is not something that is **recognised**. Self-realisation or Truth is a state of **being**. For this 'revolution' to come all thoughts of knowledge, belief or conscious effort to achieve must be put completely out of the mind. The virtuous person who is conscious of being, and staying, virtuous has not achieved self-realisation. He may be a very honest, decent and well-meaning person, but that is entirely different to the man who has found total freedom and achieved self-realisation. A virtuous man may be a righteous man but he cannot have found truth because virtue to him is consciously maintaining a certain level of self behaviour. He is, with his mind, maintaining and protecting a level of moral standards. He is **consciously** pursuing virtue. That is why Jesus said, 'blessed are the poor'. He was referring not only to the things and possessions of the world, but also to beliefs, knowledge, desires and ambitions. A man rich in worldly goods, or rich in knowledge, beliefs, teachers and scriptural information is a man far from self-realisation, but a man who will attract conflicts, doubts and misery.

He who has attained self-realisation does not understand fear. Fear only exists for the man who has beliefs, knowledge and ambitions. Fear can only exist in relation to some other things. He is, for instance, afraid of death. Death is a terrifying thought. But how can anyone be afraid of something that is totally unknown to him? Death, he knows, is inevitable, but to him it is **unknown**. So he cannot, in truth, be afraid of the unknown. But is it not a case of being afraid of losing all that is **known** to him? Or, putting it in another way, afraid of losing his association with the things he has known and in many ways possessed. The things of the world are recognisable factors which provide us with experiences which are exciting, satisfying and, at times, comforting. They give us a feeling of power and security. They give us a reputation, a character and a bank balance. It is a tangible world which is reassuring. It is a world to which we have become conditioned to, perhaps over many lives. It is a world of recognisable knowledge, beliefs, desires which can easily be satisfied, religions, opinions and ideas and it provides us with a logical sense of **continuity** in relation to all things which are known to us. Therefore, the man who is afraid is actually afraid of that which is **known** to him and so he is afraid of losing those things to which he is already attached. Two basic fears control the life of the attached man. One is the fear of losing those things to which he is attached and the other is the fear of not getting the things he desires. So when the reader seriously considers the above he will realise that the **unknown** is the **reality** – that **Absolute** Self. The attached man is not afraid of the **total freedom** that lies deep within, simply because it is totally unknown to him.

Beliefs can create many fears. All religions are an accumulation of beliefs. Preachers instil, into all religiously attached people, beliefs concerning the saving graces of Jesus, Buddha, Krishna and other masters. People cling to these beliefs which become images and they pray to these images because it gives them a feeling of comfort and a sense of security. When things threaten to go wrong or there is a possibility of losing someone dear to them, or if there comes a need for self-protection, they appeal to one of these images. Even though they have no absolute knowledge or concrete proof of the reality of their beliefs, many are afraid of losing the beliefs and are very much afraid of anything, or anyone, who is likely to disturb or weaken their faith in the belief. Fear always exists during the accumulation of things and beliefs. Desire and belief in **anything** is part of the accumulation process, therefore there is also fear during the process and afterwards. Whenever man accumulates things outwardly, he also accumulates conflicting emotions including greed, anger, jealousy, envy selfishness and suspicion. On the other hand, when he accumulates **inwardly**, that is via the mind, he accumulates beliefs, knowledge, methods and dogmas which create the same pains and doubts. Therefore fear of the unknown is really fear of losing the accumulated knowledge of things, beliefs and other attachments. Fear also comes when we live in accordance with a particular set way of living. This pattern of living is, in truth, an attachment to pre-established thoughts, to things, a particular order of service, a style of accommodation and comfort. Fear, or conflict, also arises when we fail to achieve a certain standard which we have already formulated in the mind. If a person demands a certain standard of living, respect or acknowledgement, that also is a display of fear. The enlightened person who is familiar with the nature of the world and the nature of man, is a person who lives without fear because he is not aroused by any particular way which lies outside. He is conscious only of one way and that all other ways are illusionary, superficial, temporal and therefore of the ego-mind. Should the reader, at this particular point, suddenly decide that he must, at all costs, change his particular pattern because he **wants** to be free of fear, then he is merely changing his pattern of life for another which will continue to create other fears according to the new pattern. The reader should bring to mind that any **desire** to **change** is merely changing the conditions, but the conditions of the outside still remain. How then does he become free of the fears if he cannot change the conditions? First of all, remember that every **act** to change the conditions will create no changes concerning the **source** of the fears. Every act must be considered as a **physical** attempt because thoughts can be physical things. The reader must stop and think, meditate if he wishes, until he comes to the realisation that the mind itself **is the pattern**. Every form of desire is an addiction created by the mind. The mind itself is the fear which it was created and, therefore, it is experiencing itself. So, by attempting to use **this** mind one is simply re-creating (perhaps different conditions but equally conflicting) with the same material, the same desires, the same actions and reactions and the same fears.

CHAPTER FIVE

THE NATURE OF THE MIND

Why does nearly everything in life involve us in problems? The whole business of living, money, work, relationships, religion and earning a living always gives rise to some problem. Why is earth life, and only earth life, always fraught with difficulties and fears? In spite of incredible technological advances which are designed to make life better in the home, in the workshops, places of leisure and in medical centres, there always remains the feeling of **wanting** – a feeling of insufficiency. We never seem to achieve total satisfaction. In spite of the advances of medical science there still remains much evidence of illness, disease, mental illness, stress and unhappiness. Disease, or the possibility of disease, is uppermost in the minds of many people. Would it be because we, the citizens, and the scientists think and act from the same viewpoint? That is, from the same fixed point of observation, action and reaction? We are always thinking from the intellectual, or earth-mind, point of view, to the outer point of action. In other words, we are dependent upon the periphery, or ego-mind, for results.

The periphery is often referred to as the superficial world. Everything in it is superficial. Therefore all reactions, or returns, are superficial. The **vital** man is not superficial. The **vital** life involves the '**Whole Man**', body, mind, the deeper inner-consciousness or Absolute Self. Most people live only from the body and mind. This is bound to be superficial because they are only living from the **part-man**, that part that is always thinking from and to the periphery. Therefore, everything that is created from the periphery is a problem because we are living in the superficial. Problems, fears and wanting are synonymous with the superficial. So long as we live in the field of the superficial mind we will continue to experience complications, problems and illusions. On the other hand when we live and think from the 'Centre', or deep inner-self, everything looks different, the returns are different, because when you live from the Centre you are thinking from the **Whole-Man**. From the Centre nobody dies, nobody can die, because death does not exist. But when you live from the periphery you die and everybody else dies. Death is the natural result of all action which takes place in the superficial world because there there is no eternal life. The superficial world is as permanent as a beefburger. How can something eternal be found in a temporal world? The superficial, or earth-mind is sensation. This mind is in being only because it is the result of **accumulated** sensations and reactions. It can never fail to recall the enjoyment of a beefburger, but misery and emptiness always follow the enjoyment because the beefburger, symbolic of all sensual things, has a short life and therefore only affords a limited experience. Sensual objects are part of the periphery and every aspect of the periphery must die sooner or later. However, the problem of the misery is not to be found in the periphery itself, but always in the mind that created it. The mind will work slavishly for us night and day, but the mind is the most superficial of all things, the sole creator of all our problems and conflicts. It recognises only those things which are temporal and to these things it attaches itself. The inevitable result is that we are hurt, become frightened and frustrated when the things turn out to be temporal. Concentrate upon the thought that man, which means you, is an **eternal**, spiritual being. The eternal man cannot die, only the body with its mind of accumulated senses dies. It has died many times and it will die every time it is attracted to and becomes a part of the sense world. This basic law of attraction is the fundamental influence which brings into being the law of reincarnation.

There will eventually come the time when you will stop dying. That time will be when you overcome the desires of the senses, lose the desire to look outwards and begin to turn the thoughts inward to the inner being. Only then does the superficial mind die. Ironically, we have spent a whole life, many lives, cultivating this mind, making it more and more demanding, stronger and more subtle. The very nature of this mind is such that it can only become more cunning, dishonest, deceptive and incapable of facing truth. These are the things which not only create our problems and conflicts, but **are** the problems. What really is a problem, why is it a problem and what does a problem do? As already stated, a problem can only be associated with the things of the superficial world. Nothing else can be associated with problems. Let us take, for example, one particular problem which is the drinking of alcohol. Is it the **act** of drinking or is it the **thought** behind the drinking which is the problem? It cannot possibly be the act which is the problem simply because the act comes **after** the thought. If you are thinking about drinking alcohol, or anything else, all day because the desire is always in the mind then that is the problem. Now, ask yourself, is it the act of drinking which is the problem or is it the thought before the act? Now, why do you hold on to the thought? Why is it the central issue in your life when there are so many other things demanding your attention? The mind chooses to occupy itself with this particular thought because it is the ultimate escape. It is one way of forgetting the **self-mind** with its accumulation of responsibilities and duties concerning the many things of the world. These things, which are really a combination of desires and ambitions, can be so frustrating, so elusive, so difficult to hold for any length of time. In order to achieve and secure these impossible things the mind can become dishonest, deceitful and even aggressive. Through the acquired habit of drinking, over-eating, sex or drug-taking, for the time being, for those few moments, one is able to forget the burden of the outside world. The mind knows of no other way of escaping or forgetting the **accumulation** within itself. Everything else in life gives seeming 'reality' or emphasis to the accumulated-mind. Your job, the bank balance, family responsibilities, social commitments, unfulfilled ambitions and various desires all give emphasis and power to the mind.

Therefore, this one act of drinking, sex or drugs produces a moment of **self-forgetfulness**. This one moment offers a convenient avenue of complete forgetfulness. Just for a moment you are free, you are happy. Everything else **outside** of that moment is a nightmare, a source of fear and pain. So you cling to that moment for as long as possible, or repeat the moment as often as possible. This moment of joyfulness of the mind is mistaken for happiness. In time, gradually, there develops the thought, a most disturbing thought, that you have become a slave to the habit. This is just one more conflict, another fear to be added to the others. The actual acts of drinking, over-eating, sex or drug-taking are in themselves not the problems. Once the act is committed, one can say, the horse has already bolted, but the subsequent troublesome thoughts concerning the recurring act **are** the problem. So the mind decides to do something about it. It begins to practise different methods, all to do with preventing the act happening again. But all that happens is that that new method becomes a new addiction because these methods are simply **mental** operations created by the very mind which created the act in the first place. All acts which have become habitual, whether involving drugs, drink, sex, smoking or over-eating are the **same** problems and any new methods adopted to overcome the disturbing acts are a part of the same problem. This is because the problem **is** the mind, not the act or the preventative method.

Habitual acts will always remain a difficult and complex problem as long as we remain ignorant of the nature of the mind which thinks about, or desires, and thereby creates the problem. It cannot be emphasised enough that the physical act is not the problem, only the urging thought behind the act. All acts are only the physical reactions of the accumulated mind. Of course, it is possible, through concentration and thought, to suppress a particular addiction, but this one accomplishment does not overcome the **source** of all other addictions or attachments, because the source is the **entire** accumulated mind. The source can only be overcome when we fully understand the nature of the **'me'** or, **'this-is-mine'** mind. To overcome the drinking problem, for example, is only one small achievement over a mind which has been totally free to accumulate information and the experiences of countless superficial incidents; a single drop taken out of the ocean as it were. As long as the mind is free to pursue ambitions, lust after power, riches and authority and feed greedily upon the things of the world you will continue to experience all the problems of the superficial world, such as fear, suspicion, anger, doubt, insecurity and jealousy. In return the mind will continue to find many ways for moments of self-forgetfulness. The life of the troubled man is, in reality, a life of contradiction. First there is the emphasis on the ego-self which accumulates the superficial things, then comes the emphasis on the various methods to lose himself for a few moments in order to escape from the problems of 'thing-attachment'. This state of contradiction is the basic reason why life is so complex and appears to be almost impossible to understand. Finding satisfactory avenues of escape is even more difficult and frustrating. There are many well-meaning persons who earnestly desire a settled, tranquil life, but in spite of their many good, even spiritual, efforts life becomes too often a nightmare. They become confused, frustrated and often bitter because of the seeming injustices. The problem is, again, the life of contradiction. In all good faith they acquire and work for things which they believe are necessary for a comfortable life. They have failed to recognise the way of attachment. The dual-state of contradiction cannot be solved by the mind because the mind itself is the problem, is the state of contradiction. The state of contradiction can only be understood when one understands the 'Whole-Man', including the whole purpose of life, the whole nature of man, the whole nature of the world and the relationship of the mind of man to the things of the world. Man has spent all his life, many lives in fact, looking through the wrong end of a fixed telescope. He has come to believe that all he sees is the whole, the reality. Only a few, the mystics, prophets, gurus and masters have learned how to turn the telescope around and look deep into the inner world. These are the few who experience the unchanging tranquil life. They **observe** problems but are not a part of them. They are the few without ambitions, spiritual or otherwise, therefore they experience no problems. This can only happen when the self is forgotten, when the 'this is mine' attitude is non-existent. The 'this is mine' mind exists only as long as we are dependent upon reactions. The acts of drinking, smoking and drug taking, etc., are merely **reactions** to demands made by the accumulated mind.

Enlightenment, or self-realisation, can never be a reaction to some method, technique or practice. Enlightenment is not, and never can be an act of will. The addictive acts are only reactions which arise when the mind tries to overcome a problem or mind conflict. When the mind attempts to solve a problem in this way it can only add to the problem, creating more confusion and frustration. I cannot emphasise enough that the actual act is not the problem. The mind is the problem. All the mind can do is suppress the problem, or problems. But suppression is but a momentary solution. It is impossible for the mind to cultivate anything of a spiritual nature within the character of a person. Spirituality cannot be cultivated any more than intuition, inspiration, compassion, kindness or love can be cultivated. Skills can be cultivated but spirituality is not a skill, something that can be learned. For example, the man who is trying to cultivate humility cannot be humble. Many of man's problems are created by the mind safeguarding his pride, dignity and sense of authority. All of these emotions are directly opposed to humility. Humility is not a thing of the mind. No one can decide to become humble, but you can decide to become anything you wish providing it is **of** the mind. If there is love within your soul then you will be humble and compassionate. Like humility, love is not a thing of the mind. Therefore, all problems concerning the activities of self and the efforts of the mind to escape the conflicts, by creating moments of self-forgetfulness, can only be overcome when the nature of the mind is fully understood.

Of course we cannot stop ourselves from thinking but, nonetheless conflicts come to an end when the self (earth-mind) stops thinking about itself. The self only comes into being because of the attractions of the superficial world. Attractions create the attachment and the thought. The self having created an identity, or character, because of its attachment to the superficial world means, obviously, that the identity or character is illusionary because the things themselves are illusionary. When the time comes and there is a total realisation of this illusionary factor, then, and only then, does thought become a reality or fact. This must happen because eventually the old thought patterns of the mind come to an end. Only then those who created repetitive acts, because they craved moments of self-forgetfulness, realise that these problems of old can be eliminated. Only then will they realise that the addictions were the only things to which the mind gave predominance. Whenever the mind gives predominance to anything it automatically becomes a problem and a conflict.

It must be clearly understood that the mind does have its proper place in our life. Mind in its proper place, when it is thoroughly understood, is seen to be neither good, bad, evil, pure, impure or addictive. When the mind finds it difficult to exist without some particular kind of happiness or excitement then it is a problem. For example, food and drink are essential to the existence and well being of the body, but when food and drink become objects of sensual pleasure then this means that the mind is in the wrong place. Money is important when it is used to buy the essential things to maintain life on a reasonably comfortable level, but when it is used to build giant empires, create monopolies, because the mind is in the wrong place, money creates considerable conflicts and problems. Therefore, when mind understands, recognises and accepts its proper place, the process of conflict comes to an end. This is not offered as a convenient answer to the problems of daily or community life, it is the one and **only** answer because the mind denies spiritual love. It accepts only sensual love and where there is no spiritual love only then does the mind create problems.

Why can we be sure that spiritual love is denied by the mind? Because we already know that spiritual love is the **unknown**. That is, unknown to the mind. Spiritual love can be realised but only by discarding that which is **known** and by this we mean the mind. Before spiritual love can be realised it must first be discovered, but that which is **unknown** cannot possibly be discovered by the mind of knowing. So the first thing we must do is to examine the nature of the known by the process of experience. However, we must consider and analyse our findings of the known without any feelings of condemnation, fear or judgement of any kind. Only then can we take steps, difficult steps indeed, to free the mind from its accumulation of facts, knowledge, information, addictions and beliefs because the mind will have (eventually) fully realised the true nature of itself. Before, the mind was in a complete state of ignorance regarding its real nature – now it is free.

CHAPTER SIX

FINDING YOURSELF IN A QUIET ROOM

What is enlightenment? It is said that mystics and Masters are enlightened but what is the fundamental difference between us ordinary people and the mystics? Almost everyone would like to be a Master or a mystic so what would they have to do or what must they learn to be a mystic? The truth is we cannot **learn** enlightenment, or, to be more exact, we cannot **know** enlightenment. Enlightenment is an **infinite** height of spiritual awareness. To **know** about something means you have come to a conclusion. A conclusion is to absorb a limited piece of knowledge. The moment you come to a conclusion, that is, to know about something, you come to a full stop. That is the problem with the intellectual mind. It continues to absorb countless bits of information. You can read all the religious books in the world but it will not enable you to experience enlightenment. Enlightenment is not knowledge, it is not dependent on information or 'knowing' about religion. Enlightenment is very subtle, it has no basis. It comes into being only when you have reached a certain spiritual development. Enlightenment comes into being when you experience and understand the way of humanity; when you have a full understanding of yourself in relation to the world of people, the nature of the world and the nature of man.

Those people who read the scriptures over and over again until they know every word, every chapter and verse are not increasing their spirituality but are really cultivating their memory. When you are completely healthy, the state of health is present, but you are quite unconscious of your body. On the other hand when something goes wrong, there is discomfort and pain and immediately and constantly you become conscious of the body. An enlightened person, likewise, is never conscious of enlightenment, no more than a saint is aware of his spirituality. Fear, anger, jealousy, material ambition, greed, etc., are sicknesses and should make us aware of the absence of enlightenment. When you are free of these things, without resistance to things and people there is no consciousness of the freedom. It is only when there is conflict, limitation and frustration that you are completely conscious of these things. These are the moments when the soul yearns for freedom and release. It is the same when you are unhappy. You long for happiness, but when you are happy, you **are** happy and you don't stop to think about it. So it is with enlightenment.

So enlightenment is an infinite height of spirituality which we cannot think about because it is far beyond the intellect, that faculty which allows us to **know** about things. Therefore, enlightenment is the **unknown**. Which means that everything that is known stands firmly between you and enlightenment. What we must do now is to discover and realise everything that is known. The mind is full of everything that is known. The mind gives prominence to everything that gives it pleasure, power, authority and importance. As all of these things are of a temporal nature, which means they eventually dissolve into nothingness, then the mind must be thought of as an illusionary entity. In other words, everything is fictitious. When eventually there develops the total realisation of this, as a truth, then the mind is no longer the dominating supervisor of every hour of your conscious day. Therefore, what we must do first is to look at that which is known. We look at it analytically, honestly and with courage. We are now entering into a form of meditation which the Zen Buddhists refer to as mind suicide.

This cannot be an easy, straightforward exercise. It will require considerable patience. Try this little experiment. Lock yourself away in a room with plenty of writing paper. Start by thinking of a beefburger. Write down everything possible about it. Why you want it. Your feelings regarding it. Every little effort required to obtain it. Bring to mind the number of minutes of enjoyment it gives you. Now contemplate the moments immediately **after** the last piece of beefburger has disappeared into your stomach. Now consider what has happened to the experience. Finally, but most important, ask yourself what has the experience accomplished for you. Then you will realise the truth that the experience, the effort and the beefburger have accomplished precisely nothing. The experience has simply created a memory which will become another part of the accumulated mind, just another attachment to the state of illusion. The memory will serve as a dictator demanding the same illusionary experience over and over again. Once again you are the little mouse running round and round the big wheel, getting nowhere, staying exactly in the same spot, but the illusionary mind makes you believe you are moving forward. Next day, try another experiment. Think of a chocolate bar and again write all your thoughts down. Another time think of an ambition. Could it be of promotion, becoming an owner of a new motor car, the supreme boss of your company, winning a great sum of money or becoming an important person in your community. Now write down why you value these things so much. At the completion of your write-up, consider whether with these things you will be able to forget the world, your worries, fears and responsibilities.

Unconscious thinking about the things of the world is like a drug and in the same way you become addicted to it. You only believe, in **your mind**, that you can forget the world and its conflicts. The truth is you are only creating a different kind of world within the mind. It is not real, but just a dream. How real is the beefburger once you have eaten it? It does not stay very long with you. Then you must replace it over and over again. Everything in the sense world, including ambition, is a beefburger. This thinking, this drug, has created a hallucinatory world and you have locked yourself within it, it has become your home. You have lived within it for so long that you have become accustomed to it. This illusionary world of thought has become a kind of reality, little realising that it is actually a prison. Even though you feel some kind of security, always believing, hoping it will get better, it is still a prison. Prisoners who have spent most of their lives in prison are always afraid of coming out. Total freedom lies outside the walls, but they are afraid of freedom because it offers something totally new – it is the **unknown**. Beyond the mind all things are unknown. The unknown is the absolute freedom. Only the mind is afraid of it because it means total death. The infinite always looks like total death to the mind because it has become accustomed to the finite – recognisable boundaries, limitations which are fully comprehensible to the mind. The mind is the supreme boss of the world of limitation. Unfortunately, there is no limit to the growth of the mind. The more thoughts, dreams and ambitions you put into the mind, the more it will grow and grow. An ordinary mind can memorise everything in the world, every library, every dream, every ambition, every religion, but every item is nothing more than a beefburger. The life-span of all things is short. Each item is a symbol of death. Even if you contain the whole world in your mind it will experience total death. Shankara (Hindu) said, 'All that you know is illusion.' Whatever you see is a reflection of the senses: whatever you touch, hear, smell, see or taste is a reflection of the senses which, in turn, are slaves of the mind. The mind is also a clever distorting mirror. The mind convinces you that whatever you have known is necessary. For instance the beefburger appears to be real because when the one is eaten and disappears into your stomach the mind tells you that there are a million more available outside. The supply will never dry up. There are a million sensual experiences; a million deaths. But it is the same beefburger, the same short-lived experience being repeated over and over again. Each experience dies leaving nothing behind but a memory held by the mind.

What you are doing during the experiments inside the locked room is finding out the values of the **known**. Looking at the problems that disturb you daily and analysing the little irritations which are attracted to you in the community, the office and the home. Carefully analyse each problem then ask yourself the question, 'Is it my pride, ego, dignity, selfishness, greed or aggressiveness which is really behind the problem'? Make no excuses for yourself, do not attempt to blame others or put the blame elsewhere. When these problems are looked at purely and courageously the mind, the known, or rather the nature of the known, becomes inwardly recognisable and so the mind is slowly released. As the process continues, so the degree of freedom gradually becomes greater.

Love, that is to love someone, can be the cause of many conflicts and problems. So now let us make love the subject of another experiment in our locked room. As before, analyse your love for a particular person. Does your love also mean possession of that person from which jealousy could arise? Does the thought of losing that person arouse fear, anger, or resentment because of the possibility of loneliness? So, now, seriously consider the nature of these feelings. First take jealousy. Jealousy is a fear; it is also lack of faith not only in the person, but in the love they have for you. Jealousy is anger, suspicion and doubt. Can these feelings possibly be a part of love? Surely it is total possession? Jealousy is aroused by thought and love is not thought. Love cannot be created through the process of thinking. Also love is not emotion or sentiment. Sentimentality, emotion and jealousy are merely forms of self-expression, or mind-expression. We already know that jealousy can be cruel, but sentimentality can also be cruel because sentiments always demand a response and if the right response is not forthcoming the sentimental or emotional person can be stirred to great anger, hatred and even violence. Therefore a person in love who can be aroused to tears or fears, is not expressing love, but fears for himself or herself. That is, fears concerning possible losses to themselves. A person who is truly and spiritually in love is indifferent to enmity, jealousy or resentment. None of these can possibly be a part of love. In fact, they are all a part of the mind. In spiritual love no part of the mind is involved. The mind cannot create love any more than it can create beauty. Furthermore, there cannot be love where there is no faith or respect. Jealousy and possession can only be manifest where there is no faith or respect. During the experiment ask yourself another question. Do you have equal respect for those who work beneath you as for those who are above you, such as the boss, the vicar, the celebrity, the millionaire or a particularly attractive person? Do you have a special language for those in the 'top' bracket and another for those in the lower bracket?

Through this experiment we can discover what spiritual love is **not** because, as love is the **unknown**, we will eventually come to the realisation of it by discarding that which is known. The unknown cannot be discovered by a mind that is full of the known. Through these experiments you will learn not to allow the things of the mind to fill the heart. When this happens there is only spiritual love. Only then will you not want to possess, not be envious, not greedy, be respectful to everyone irrespective of their position or wealth, have full consideration for your neighbour as well as for your wife and for your family as well as for your servants. Bring to mind the following thought: love cannot be cultivated by thought, by practise, by systems. In fact, anything which is of the mind cannot be love, cannot be spiritual. Only mystics and masters can say 'I love the world' simply because they know how to love one: if you can love one then you can love the whole. The mystics know only love. Most people create a specific love which is attachment. This is a mistake which nearly all people make. They do not know the difference between love and specific love. Krishna, the Christ of India, taught that there is neither one nor many: there is only love. In the Bhagavad Gita this vital truth is clearly illustrated in the parable when Krishna urges Arjuna, his disciple, onto the battlefield commanding him to slay his uncles, cousins, nephews, etc. Arjuna is filled with sorrow and asks Krishna why he must kill. Krishna replies, 'You can only kill that which is destined to die.' Krishna explains that Arjuna, in creating a special respect for his relatives, which is also a special love, has created attachments which makes his love for his family fictitious. Real love is love of humanity. Jesus taught one vital lesson, 'Love thy neighbour as thyself.' He also said, 'Love you one another.' In loving only uncles and aunts we are only loving in part. We create a specific recognition, a special love. There is also a special respect and consideration which we do not give to our neighbours. When one of our relatives is experiencing a serious problem, we go to any lengths to help him sacrificing time, money and other duties in order to bring comfort and peace of mind, but with an ordinary neighbour, who may also be in need, we consider that he or she is not our responsibility. They are the concern of others. Therefore, we do not feel duty bound to sacrifice as much, if anything at all. Aunts, uncles, cousins and nephews are things of the mind, a special relationship, which only the mind recognises. That is attachment. So we recognise in this parable that Jesus and Krishna were teaching the same truth.

Here are further experiments to be conducted in your locked room. Ask yourself the question, why is there so much pain and suffering in the world? Begin by reminding yourself that if you can find the cause of your own pain and suffering you will find the reason for so much suffering in the world because it is the same suffering. Your mind is their mind, they are the same mind. The same **known** things. There is fear of death, there is poverty, disease, the trauma of old age, starvation, failure in business and family relationships. You desperately want something but you cannot get it, so there is misery. You want more money, more recognition, so there is more misery and frustration. A loved one, or a friend, dies and there is great sadness. There is misery, pain, sadness and frustration because there is something we want and cannot get. Try to imagine the state of the world if everybody got everything they wanted. Most people become angry because they seriously believe that it is their right to have things just because they want them. Now consider all the things you want. Having concentrated on the things you want, now consider the millions, say in the Third World, who haven't got the vital things they need to sustain life. Now ask yourself why you need these things. Naturally, we need food, clothing and shelter, but are you satisfied with these or do you want more? Now ask yourself why you need more. Think carefully and deeply about this one. Do you want success, do you need more authority, more power? Do you want to be famous, respected, looked up to? Again, why do you want all this? Question yourself further, why all this craving for more and more. Are you dissatisfied, discontented, if so, with what? Are you dissatisfied with what you are? Do you believe that you would be more contented with expensive new clothes, a shining limousine, being the supreme boss, a film star! Now ask yourself the question, are the millionaire, the boss, the film star or the president supremely satisfied, contented and happy people? Or are they just covering up their discontent with expensive clothes, power, wealth and position? Are they really happy people? In most cases the dissatisfaction, the unrest, is still there. So first we must work to understand what we really are. Concentrate on what we must do. Is it enough merely to cover ourselves with money, power, beautiful clothes and everything that is of the outside? Most powerful men, with great wealth and authority, are not happy which proves that the 'coverings' are meaningless and powerless to remove our sadness. It is equally useless for these unhappy men to run after gurus, mystics and masters. These exalted persons cannot alter your mind, cannot release the known from your mind. Only you can do that. The wise man knows there is no release in his possessions or power. If it were possible for you to go deep behind the mind and look outwards, you would see that there is a great struggle going on within for you to achieve something, something that in truth is very small, empty and more important, something that is very limited. But still you struggle to achieve it. You will never achieve it because what you want to achieve is of the mind. The mind is unreal, therefore whatever you achieve you are destined to lose. So the struggle continues. The very struggle to achieve, to become something is the cause of your discontent. It is important to recognise what you are. It is important to go deeper within yourself. How can you find out about yourself? Will you know it from books? Which author will understand your problem because there are so many authors and they all have different theories and ideas? Every different person offers different ideas and suggestions as to how to achieve happiness and contentment. The hungry man just wants food, the unhealthy want health, the young wife wants a child, the poor man wants wealth, the politician wants to be president. All these people want something satisfying, comforting and providing security. But, that thing is only the beginning. It is never because having achieved the first thing, they never want something else. What they have achieved is not permanent, so they continue trying to find something permanent.

So the general goal and desire of man is embedded within you. You want hope, security, happiness and satisfaction, but the goal is the same within you as in the **entire world**. There is no difference because you are a part of the whole. So we have to find out if there is something else beyond that which is known, beyond the mind. All the illusions of the mind must be recognised. You must understand them and realise their nature. Only then can you discover the real goal. To hold on to the belief that there is something worthwhile, something real which can be achieved by the mind is simply creating another illusion. Start by questioning all your conflicts, struggles, pains, fears, frustrations, vanities, hopes and ambitions. Concentrate upon them, understand them, then go beyond. Only then will your realise that you are struggling to hold on to something that cannot be held. Recognise and accept the illusionary nature of the world and the illusionary nature of man's feelings and desires. Don't even desire God because you already **are** God.

Do you ever wonder about the soul? Have you ever questioned whether it really exists and if it actually survives the physical death? If you are advancing in years then this could create a fear. The result is that you would like to be convinced of the existence of the soul. Where and how do you start? By reading the scriptures or talking to the priest? Are these avenues convincing enough? Does the priest or any other religious leader really know, or could they be wrong? So your next question is: What is the soul? Do the scriptures or the priest describe the soul? Obviously if the soul exists then it is something way beyond the physical and the intellectual mind. So let us examine what it is. We do have something we are conscious of. Naturally, there is the physical body which expresses itself in various ways. There is our character, which every individual expresses in many different ways. It has a quality which we experience and react to. For example if the other person is reflecting a bad quality we feel hurt, angry, embarrassed or frustrated. If it is a good quality we feel love, compassion, kindness and even wisdom.

Consider the wisdom of a guru, mystic or master. Now consider yourself and contemplate the difference between yourself and the guru or the master. What makes the difference? It cannot be the flesh, the bones or the brain. The brain is merely a library. There are numerous brainy or intellectual persons about, but are they mystics or masters? The answer is clearly no. Then what creates the difference between the intellectual and the mystic or guru? If it is not the body and its organs it must be something which far transcends all this, something which the mind and brain cannot reach. We all have brains and minds, even monkeys have brains and minds, but all of us are not masters. Some people have highly developed intuition, inspiration, some have psychic gifts and others have spiritual healing gifts, but most have very little or none at all. So what creates the difference? It has to be something greater than the physical. So, we must consider another dimension entirely.

Let us search to see if there is, in fact, another dimension of life which ordinary men and women are completely unconscious of. Let us start with man himself. His body is made up of hundreds of millions of minute cells. Each cell is a complete, minute world. The sophisticated electron microscope reveals each cell as a microscopic balloon containing a jelly-like substance. In the centre there floats a nucleus. The nucleus is vital, it is the brain, the life of the cell. Remove it and the cell dies. There is a constant activity going on. A regular intake of oxygen and foodstuffs and a continuous excretion of waste matter. If the environment changes the cell will adapt itself to the change. If the cell is damaged (not too much) it will automatically repair itself. Man, himself, knows nothing of what is going on. All these cells reproduce themselves, for the purpose of developing the body, for repair work, and for growth.

When scientists look at the reproductive activity of these cells (the process of development and growth) they see a remarkable series of events. This process is to be seen in the countless millions of cells of all living things. The cell nucleus, within its own balloon-like membrane begins to undergo a miraculous change. First, within the balloon there mysteriously develops a coiled, thread-like structure. It resembles a spiral. At a certain time this spiral thread breaks up into minute segments (chromosomes) and the number of segments is precise for all humans and animals. Plants have a similar process but the number of segments are different, although, nevertheless, precise. All of these segments are the carriers for all inherent characteristics and qualities. At the same time another microscopic structure (centrosome), which has been lying dormant inside the cell, becomes active at **exactly the same time** as the spiral breaks up. Extremely fine threads, or filaments, radiate from it. The centrosome now splits into two halves which arrange themselves on either side of the nucleus. The thread-like filaments reach out and attach themselves to each minute segment or chromosome. There is a thread for each segment and once each segment is attached, the cell immediately splits up into two. So now we have two cells from one. The process continues so that the two cells become four, then eight and so on. Scientists are able to observe this remarkably accurate and precise process. Each segment and each microscopic cell knows exactly what to do, when to do it and where its exact place is. The incredible mystery is that the cell is directed by some kind of intelligence, but the intelligence is far above and beyond that of man's. The most advanced scientists, with their extremely accurate and sophisticated instruments, cannot duplicate this process. It remains a total mystery. Which proves there is a super-consciousness in charge of man and all living things. Could this super-consciousness be the soul, a cosmic intelligence, God? The only indisputable fact we have is that the process is there, working, and it is seen to be working. But no one knows how. This cell, with its even smaller segments, is the smallest unit in existence manifesting life.

Now we come to the phenomenon of death. What is death? Your next question is, do we survive death? Death is the unknown, and what matters is to know of the unknown while you are living. To help us to answer these questions, surprisingly we must turn to the scientists. There is little doubt that science and physics have placed more faith in the minds of people than religion, but on the other hand they have failed to replace hope and provide comfort damaged when a loved and dear one has died. Atomic structures and chemical formulae would find it impossible to compete with a baby's smile, the gentle touch of a lover, a partner's kiss, embrace or reassuring presence.

Nevertheless, it is highly surprising to discover how many, down-to-earth, hard-nut scientists, realists and precision thinkers suggest that consciousness, awareness, memory, personality and identity could be preserved after the death of the physical brain and body. Some suggest even more positively that it could be possible for the so-called dead to communicate through scientifically created energy channels which, they predict, will soon be established.

Alfred North Whitehead, an eminent mathematician and philosopher declared that science was blind, totally blind, because it dealt with only a small part of the evidence (for survival) provided by human experience. There was considerably more to the world of atomic structure. Matter was only the tip of the iceberg. Arthur Young, another brilliant sub-atomic physicist, totally agreed with Whitehead. He said that the 'whole-man' would never be fully understood by simply concentrating on the physical shape that made up man. There was much more to man than matter.

Werner Heisenberg, a famous German physicist, had this to say about the atomic (material) world, including the beings who inhabit it. 'Atoms are much more than things or particles. There is a higher force which proves that there is no clear distinction between matter and energy. There is some kind of intelligence.' Another well-known German physicist, Max Planck, spent many years investigating the sub-atomic realm and was compelled to state that there existed another world of reality which lay beyond our present world of sense.

Undoubtedly, one of the most startling discoveries was made by two quantum (sub-atomic) physicists, Professor Segre of Italy and Dr Chamberlain, an American scientist, who discovered the anti-proton. For their remarkable discovery they were awarded the Nobel Prize for physics in 1959, in Stockholm. Our present sense (material) world is constructed of protons and electrons which form the atom. Discovering the anti-proton meant that the scientifically established proton now exists in **two** separate forms: 1. protons with mass (touchable matter); and 2. anti-protons (anti-mass). In other words, a structure which lies beyond the sense-touch of man. Which means that anti-matter is now established. Therefore, the world we now see consists of the normal atomic structure, but within that sense world there exists a sub-atomic world. In other words, a non-mass world interpenetrating our normal sense world, or world of mass. Many years earlier two famous British scientists, Sir Oliver Lodge and Sir William Crookes, President of the British Association for the Advancement of Science, made similar discoveries and came to the conclusion that proof of the survival of the soul will be found in the sub-atomic world – the world of anti-matter.

Arthur Young went even further in his life-long study and investigations into the world of anti-matter. Young was quite certain that there was a definite connection between the sub-atomic world (anti-matter) and **consciousness**. The phenomenon of light had always remained a total mystery to all scientists. Little was known about this phenomenon. So Arthur Young devoted a considerable number of years to this strange, least understood, phenomenon of light. Light, he knew, was without mass (normal atomic structure). Light is similar to colour in that it is also without mass. For instance, colour must be provided with a vehicle of mass in order to manifest, for example, a flower, paint, dye or liquid. Obviously, one cannot imagine colour without a vehicle. Therefore, colour is without mass. Yet, we cannot deny that it is there, because we can see it. Light is also without mass and without charge or energy, yet Young proves, it is capable of creating protons and electrons with charge and energy. Young, now realising that he was on the verge of something outstanding and revolutionary, pursued his experiments because he believed that there was something else, some yet unknown element present. Then he discovered the photon. A photon, he realised, was a pulse, similar to light, which had no mass and no charge. Which proved, once again, that two different worlds existed together, one matter and the other anti-matter.

Into this truly breathtaking, remarkable and psychic discovery steps the greatest of all physicists, Albert Einstein. Einstein proved the photons actually existed, **but they do not exist in time**. In other words, they do not recognise time because time is of **our** dimension – the dimension which defines matter. He also proved that **everything** in existence, both in the world of matter and anti-matter, is based upon photons. The photon is infinite and therefore has an infinite lifetime. Therefore, our bodies for instance, are simply composed of forms of light, or photons; a whole system of photons. These photons can take any form they wish, as mass and anti-mass. Thus Einstein was able to state that as the photons of anti-mass were integral with consciousness, therefore, on this basis consciousness would continue after the death of the **physical** brain. As the memory bank, our awareness and identity are part of the consciousness, so they also must survive the physical death.

The anti-proton, or photon, which has no mass, no charge and an infinite lifetime, is now established as the vital bridge between the state of being, **now**, and the state of **not being** in the physical world. Einstein went on to say that we know every particle of DNA contains the entire programme for a human being, so each particle of photon, with a infinite life-span, represents the pattern for every particle of creation not only in the universe, but in the world beyond our senses.

If we can accept the findings of some of the world's most eminent scientists (there are many other names we have not mentioned) then we must accept that there is another existence beyond this world we know. Our consciousness, awareness, memory bank, personality and identity are the factors to which together we give the name, Soul. Therefore, on the evidence provided, not by a special, confined group of scientists, but by a large number of individual scientists working alone, independently, at different times and different places, we must accept that there is no death and the vehicle which conveys our identity to another world of frequency, to function through an infinite lifetime, is the soul.

CHAPTER SEVEN

THE VITAL LAW OF OPPOSITES

For the greater part of this book I have stressed that at the true centre of man lies the divine essence, infinite and eternal wisdom, truth, love, beauty and perfection. Yet, as we look at the ever-moving pageant of human lives, we observe inequalities as strange and as inexplicable as the mystery of life itself. For hundreds of thousands of years an endless procession of human beings has come out of the unknown, briefly experienced a life that is known, only to disappear into an unknown past. Each of these passing human beings possessed hopes, dreams, fears and love. What is the purpose and the plan behind all this? When we consider the existence of individuals, we observe most people caught up in a pattern of life from which they cannot escape. All are searching for happiness, but very few know how to find it, or where to look for it. For many, too many, life is an endless struggle against despair, fear, hunger, handicap and suffering. For others fortune favours them in every way. They enjoy good health, wealth, sound minds, favourable circumstances and the joy of friendships. Has all this meaning, purpose and plan? It seems, for the whole of humanity, suffering outweighs happiness. It seems that tragedy strikes where no precaution or vigilance could have averted its consequences. Is it, therefore, any wonder that many ask the question, 'Are we the playthings of destiny, the sport of the gods? Others ask, 'Is there a cosmic order and is it fundamentally favourable to every individual?

There are many who find this cosmic plan, if it exists, meaningless. For they say, 'If God is perfect, if God is **all**, if He is central to every human being and we in our absolute essence are part of that central self, if the divine glory in each is divine, therefore infinite and eternal, what is the point of the purpose of us who are caught up in a routine from which we cannot escape? A routine not of our own choosing, but still a routine from which we try every avenue in an endeavour to escape. Why are we conditioned by an environment the nature and purpose of which we do not understand, while the harshness of its experiences appear to be inescapable? The longer we reflect upon these experiences, the more overwhelming appears the limitation of things and the more limited our areas of freedom. There is much talk of progression and soul development. If progression is an essential part of the plan and the absolute centre of man (God) is perfect, why is it necessary for the absolute to progress? Let us consider this point in some depth. If the absolute is perfect, why should perfection be thought of as a static state? Surely, it must be thought of as dynamic **life**. Divine perfection cannot be thought of as **finite** perfection. Divine perfection is the perfection of the **infinite**. Whilst we admit to the existence of finite perfection, it is feasible to accept that infinite perfection must include **all** finite possibilities.

As we examine the spectrum of differing qualities of consciousness found in the human race, there is a point where there seems to manifest a kind of primitive consciousness. Here there is virtually no sense of self. The being is just a centre almost automatically responsive to the actions and impressions of others. There is not a sufficiently developed sense of awareness to prompt planned or co-ordinated movements. A baby or very young child reveals this type of response. They are animated by sounds or actions which have the simplest of meaning because the child has a limited repertoire of actions. This is a normal and natural development because the child's mind association with environment and people has been limited. This also explains why very primitive tribes, whose total exclusion from all forms of civilisation and whose living habits are restricted to specialised and very confined areas, exhibit a simple form of consciousness. The next quality of consciousness may be called self-awareness. This develops through the natural state of association of mind with matter, environment and prevailing circumstances.

The first stage of the development of self-hood is accompanied by a sense of insecurity, a subtle sense of fear which provokes the growth of the instinct of self preservation. By processes of attitudes and responses, which are wholly self-centred, provoked by the preservation instinct, man builds up an ego-self. The ego comes into being through the instinctive need for security, safety, comfort and authority or power. The world of things is there for him to possess and use as an insurance against deterioration of his life or living standards. Instinctively aware that all human beings are involved in the same struggle for survival, he is prepared for all forms of resistance which must be fought and overcome. These basic emotions provide the physical and mental actions from which, inevitably, arise those conflicts which are characterised as selfishness, greed, suspicion, jealousy and lust for power. This particular phase of struggle and conflict may be regarded as a vital stage in the great cycle of the evolution of the soul. As the reader proceeds through these pages he will recognise this stage as the descending arc which, when the soul is at its lowest depth, experiences and absorbs as **real** every aspect and phase of the 'opposites' to reality and all that is infinite. Mystics and masters regarded this descending arc of activity as the important stage for the individualising of the ego-consciousness. At these lowest depths of consciousness all that is negative (later recognised by the higher levels of consciousness as the finite) is regarded as real and essential to the body's continuance.

Deeply immersed in a world of objects there is little doubt that the inevitable emotions and conflicts provide the 'survival-forces' and the struggles and conflicts which we characterise as selfishness, greed and possessiveness (from a more evolved point of view) are part and parcel of the Great Scheme of the soul's ultimate deliverance. Before we can build a sturdy, safe house, we must commence by establishing a firm foundation. The evolvement from simple to self-consciousness results in the establishment of the ego-consciousness. This is the foundation from which the self can contemplate its existence and evolutionise self-identity. The object or purpose of our incarnation in this grosser body is that it may by hindrance and limitation, by exercise and effort eventually attain **individual** self-awareness so that all its actions may be self-determined.

Perhaps a better explanation of the whole process of evolution is that God's plan included embryonic (or incomplete embryos) spiritual beings with a basic consciousness, but nevertheless, infinite and eternal. The plan allows the maturing of these embryos so that they come to know the divinity which they already possess, but do not realise. A constant life of confinement, limitation and struggle slowly gives an intensity and an explosive energy to life and a decisiveness and powerful urge to individuality, the absence of which would give no purpose to the plan of evolution. Concerning the gross world of consciousness at the lower end of the arc, the soul's bodily prison of limitation and illusion, Edward Carpenter in his book, **The Drama of Love and Death'** says:

> 'The devil - diabolos the slanderer and the sunderer, the principle of division - reigns. He builds up the actual, fascinating, tragic, indispensable world that we know. Selfishness and Ignorance, the two great powers of discord and separation are his ministers; the earth is his theatre of convulsive hatreds and soul-racking passion. But this diabolonian process is only one segment of the whole. After the long descent condensation and imprisonment of the spirit in its most limited, inert and self-regarding forms, after its saturation in matter, and its banishment into the world of death and suffering, the rising curve of liberation sets in, and the long process of its return. It is through love mainly that this second process works itself out. From point to point through unison with others, by absorbing something from their experiences, by sharing a wider life, the spirit's manifestation grows. Each soul is a gradual rising to consciousness of the All-Soul; a gradual liberation and self-discovery of the Divine Germ within it . . . Love indicates immortality. No sooner dies the human being, perceiving the divine nucleus within himself, than he knows his eternal destiny. Plunged into matter and the gross body he has

learned the lesson of identity and separation. All that the devil can teach him, he has faithfully absorbed. Now he has to expand that identity, for ever unique into vaster spheres of activity – to become finally a complete and finished aspect of THE ONE!'

C. C. Massey in his book, **Thoughts of a Modern Mystic** in similar terms refers to the evolutionary cycle in this way:

'The object of the embodiment of the spirit in matter is presumably that it may, by exercise and effort, attain to individual self-conscious mastery, so that all its actions may be self-determined and no longer due to automatic or involuntary response to suggestions preceding from the spirit's environment; [meaning material senses] . . . What distinguishes Spirit from Matter is that one is an active, the other a passive principle. The active principle evolves and emerges by **itself disengaging itself** from the passive principle in which it is at first bound up and imprisoned. It escapes successively by **its own activity**.'

Oneness with the All has always been a reality, but it is the state of individuality which created that 'apartness' from its Creator. Apartness is an illusion created by this temporal imprisonment in time and matter. Evolvement is a slow but progressive elimination of the illusions (apartness) so that the sense of oneness with all becomes a permanent possession. Before this can come into being the embryo spirit must gather to itself innumerable experiences and express them in countless forms continuously experiencing the actions and reactions, suffering the same, before it attains the perfect wisdom and the infinite reality. Once these are attained the soul takes on divine consciousness as it enters into the Supreme Thought, becoming an inseparable part of the Whole.

Should the reader confess to some confusion concerning the imperfections of his manner of representation of the soul's way and manner of progression, I am tempted to invite him to look for the truth from another direction. If he still admits to the cosmic process being meaningless and unnecessary I ask him to contemplate long and carefully the following imaginary illustration. Create in your mind a picture of a room. The room is without doors and windows so that there is no possible access to the outside world. In fact, in this case, no outside world exists. The room is exquisitely beautiful and everything in it reflects the elegance of absolute perfection. All requirements to sustain a calm, untroubled lifestyle in a manner that requires no physical or mental efforts are instantly available. Create this scene vividly in your mind. Contemplate it for some moments then add to this perfection the knowledge that only the power of thought is sufficient to remove, instantly, the senses of hunger and thirst. Once again I ask the reader to contemplate this situation. Remember, no action is needed, there is nothing to achieve because the extremely beautiful surroundings and the perfection of everything around you provides, automatically, all necessities. Now, contemplate for some moments that pattern of lifestyle. Then ask yourself the question, how long could you sustain that way of living? Remember, you have everything around you which is absolutely perfect and beautiful. Everything represents total security. The sense of 'wanting' is never present, therefore there is no sense of fear, no cause for conflicts. Would the unchanging observation of beauty and perfection be sufficient? Would the total freedom from action and achievement be permanently satisfying? For a while your answer may be yes. But in the long term, for the rest of your life, consider whether the answer would be the same. Obviously, it would not. The simple explanation is that the beauty and perfection are all on the outside and you remain completely unaware of the Divine Splendour, the Reality **within** yourself.

Now let us change the situation within the room. It is the same exquisitely beautiful room, the same absolute state of perfection. The only difference we make is that a new-born baby is placed in the room. All the necessary requirements for its wellbeing, comfort and maintenance of health are immediately and perfectly met. The child grows up, a perfect specimen of adulthood. The child, you must recall, has never been outside the room because there is no way out. Now, again, it is necessary for the reader to contemplate the situation deeply. Soon you will arrive at the conclusion that beauty and perfection would have no meaning, no significance in the mind of the child. Still confused? How is it that you appreciate, and enjoy, things of beauty and perfection? Could it be that you have already experienced the 'opposites' of these manifestations and you were saddened by them?

Upon reading in the Old Testament the story of Adam and Eve many thinkers have remarked upon the improbability and impracticability of such a parable. Most failed to find any significance or useful guidance and simply dismissed the reference as a fairy tale. However, as we look a little deeper into this story there is a startling resemblance to our previous story of the perfect room and the same truths are to be found. The story begins in the Garden of Eden. The perfect garden of many beautiful fruit trees. Each item of fruit was perfect and exquisite to the taste. There was an absolute abundance of this glorious fruit and it was free for the taking. Then God breathed and from the earth the image of Adam was created. The significant point to note is that God **breathed** and there was the creation of Adam. Therefore, Adam is the **breath** of God – **the life**! He was also the masculine aspect, or the First Principle – **the life**! Life, like the phenomenon of colour, must have a vehicle of expression. Life (like colour) cannot manifest by itself. It must have a means of expression. So the Bible tells us, from the lower left rib (the heart region) God created Eve. Eve, the Second Principle, the Feminine aspect – the vehicle for expression of life. In other words, Eve was the Soul. Life is a compendium of acts, expressions, feelings, emotions and desires. Life expresses these reflections through its vehicle, the Soul, as colour reflects itself through its vehicle, the flower, etc. The soul is also the vehicle for expressing the different levels of consciousness. The soul dwelling in the grosser levels will reflect that quality of consciousness which will outwardly reveal itself as cruelty, hate, selfishness and all the other lower levels of emotion. From the higher levels the soul pays tribute to the ideals of love, compassion, unselfishness, kindliness, self-sacrifice and generosity. With the appearance of Eve now Adam has an identity, a means of expression. At this point remind yourself that Adam and Eve are residing in the Garden of Perfection (the perfect room). This is not the world of opposites; there is only one state, the state of perfection. There is one vital difference between the perfect room mentioned before and the perfect garden. The perfect room had no access to the outside world. God in His wisdom provided access to the outside world from the perfect garden. There was, in fact, a forbidden area. In that area was a Tree of Knowledge which they were forbidden to touch or eat of its fruit. Eve went into the forbidden area and there was tempted, by a serpent, to take an apple. Eve accepted the apple which she offered to Adam who took a bite from it. They were immediately expelled from the Garden of Perfection.

The serpent has a specific meaning here. The serpent is symbolic of the twin powers, good and evil. It also has another name which Zen philosophy refers to as 'Kundalini'. However, we will leave that teaching until later whilst we continue our story of Adam and Eve. The Tree of Knowledge also has a special significance. In a previous chapter we state that knowledge is of the mind. Mind is a collection of information concerning the **outside** world. Mind belongs to the world of opposites. Bear it in your mind that Adam and Eve were born in a place of absolute perfection. There are no laws of opposites. In other words there is no awareness of good or evil, no negative or positive, wisdom or ignorance. Adam and Eve could not recognise good or evil because in their minds they did not exist. By entering the forbidden area the sense of curiosity was created. Being tempted to eat of the forbidden fruit (even though the garden was full of perfect fruit) created a sensual awareness, or experience, which immediately expelled them into the world of opposites which is **outside** the perfect garden. The senses, having been awakened, demanded more and more satisfaction and so the sense of desire was created which meant that attachment to the things of the outside world was also created.

Whilst contemplating the story of Adam and Eve you should realise that it is also the story of ourselves. Each of us was created from the Centre (the perfect garden), the state of perfection which does not realise or understand perfection. Not being of the world of opposites it knows nothing of good or evil, negative or positive. It is a world without manifestation, without the need for achievement because everything is perfect. There is nothing to achieve. In this world of problems it is not the world which is the problem. You and I are the problem because this world, our individual world, is the projection of ourselves. We are not separate from the world, we **are** the world and our problems are projected onto the world. Problems can only be created by mind. The world does not possess a mind.

Adam and Eve were not rejected by accident. They had to discover the nature of their minds (themselves) and the only way to discover was by learning about everything their minds were **not**. Before rejection they were **just** perfection, everything around them was **just** perfection, but perfection without understanding. There was no imperfection so how could they know perfection? There was no attachment so how could they know detachment. Ironically, in their state of perfection there existed much ignorance. Ignorance concerning the opposites. So in their ignorance of the opposites they accepted the apple thereby creating desire and attachment. When, in time, they overcome desire and attachment it will be because of their **knowledge** of desire and attachment. Desire and attachment mean struggle and conflict and, eventually, from these two aspects will arise the wisdom of peace, harmony and love. So the process of (first) individualisation is effected by struggle and conflict, commencing with ignorance of the opposites, then self-assertion, desire and selfishness. This is regarded as the descending arc in the great cycle of becoming the **Whole-Self**. The Whole-Self is the coming together of **both** wisdoms the **passive** (matter) and the **active** (spirit). The wisdom of God is not just good, positive, wisdom and love, it is **also** bad, negative, ignorance and evil. So, Adam and Eve (symbolic of ourselves, spirit and soul) are inexorably drawn down to the lowest depths of consciousness until individualised selfconsciousness has been established, then the long, very slow climb up the ascending arc begins. All that was collected, treasured and thought of as real will be slowly and painfully sacrificed as the nature of the 'things' will be recognised as negative, unreal and the cause of attachment. During the ascent the terms, good and evil, love and hate, negative and positive will be recognised as relative terms belonging solely to the world of opposites.

Our life is a series of actions at different levels of consciousness. Consciousness is challenging and reaction, which is experiencing. Experiencing is learning and recording. Thought is action and whenever we pursue action on one level of consciousness, meaning the outer, this always and unavoidably leads to conflict, struggle and frustration. Though the way of action is said to be contrary to the life of contemplation there is a certain point on the descending arc where we have no alternative but merely to act. No complete escape is possible. All actions, whether physical or mental, inevitably bring their trains of consequences and then further action is demanded of us. One action leads to another but as it is written that **all** actions originate in the Supreme Spirit, which is imperishable, inevitably there follows the sacrificial actions in which the all-pervading Spirit is constantly present.

The fact is that if all the difficulties arising from the opposites were removed, it is difficult to see how any improvements to the soul-character could come about. Without these oppositions in nature and life, nothing would have taken place. In the perfect garden, there is no significance, no meaning or purpose, we would all be sunk in a motiveless, motionless sea of stagnation. According to Buddhist philosophy there are two ways of action. One involves the renunciation of the 'fruits of action'. That is not to work and absorb the rewards for self. That way leads to struggle and conflict as observed when Adam accepted the apple and ate it. The other way of action is the way of expansion by loving devotion to humanity, therefore God. But **first** we must enter into the world of opposites, by way of the perfect garden (the Centre) partaking of its fruits. Then, by the way of fear, conflict, struggle and desire, return to the garden by way of love and understanding, having learned the bitter lesson of attachment to the fruits of our action. Such a soul is no longer entangled in a world of desire and action.

The relationship between man and what he calls the outside world is substantially a relation of mind to 'mental' objects. The desired objects of the world must, therefore, be regarded as originating in a mental field wholly sustained by the Divine Mind. The Divine Mind being the power behind all things.

The finite mind has its limited measure of creatability but because of man's present stage of development it is naturally confined to a material level. Man can create objects, but the material, or substance, used are already in existence because of Divine Intelligence. Though man is capable of expressing the 'thought-form' through the use of matter (according to acquired sense-data) it would be impossible for the same man to create an object having permanence or infinite substantiality by the process of thought alone. Therefore, we must accept that man's mind is not the highest level of the great scheme of evolutionary processes.

Man builds up an individualised consciousness (or ego) by a continuous series of attitudes, actions, reactions and processes purely for his own security, comfort or power which are wholly self-centred. If he encounters any discomforts or resistances to his ambitions then he considers that they are there to be fought against and overpowered. The emotions which provide him with the necessary driving forces can be greed, lust for power, fear, possessiveness, jealousy or selfishness.

This first, but necessary, stage of establishing an individualised ego is thought to be the **descending** curve in the great cycle of ultimate enlightenment. The complete cycle of 'becoming' obviously encompasses **embryonic** spiritual beings. In other words, Divine Beings, but at their present stage of development, experiencing simple levels of consciousness. The long, and seemingly endless, development of these souls is part and parcel of the whole scheme of development.

In essence, the vital Divine Plan is no less than the total

experiencing and suffering of the **finite** level in order to realise **infinity**, to realise immortality through the pain of mortality, to realise their omnipresence through limitation.

The apparent endless descent of the spirit into the limitations of darkness, ignorance, attachment to the illusion of matter and, thereafter, the slow ascent in which Truth, Love, Omnipresence and the Divinity of Self is realised means that the thoughts which on the descending curve were considered good and necessary now become aspects of ignorance, illusion and evil and have to be discarded.

Therefore, every soul no matter how lowly it may be considered is a master in the making. Every soul experiences the great arc of descent into gross levels of consciousness and, in turn, will experience the return to the Cosmic Consciousness. Therefore, when the scriptures record the experiences and achievements of the great teachers, masters and disciples, read them as being your experiences and the characters as being yourself. Jesus, for instance, experienced the struggle with pain, anger, fear and frustration. Everyman is a Jesus as everyman experiences the struggle on earth. Christ is not a person or personality but the attainment, symbolising the great victory over the attachment to illusion and the suffering and conflicts it brought. Christ means the Anointed One, the Divine Appointment to the Realm of the Absolute Spirit. The Bible, as with all the scriptures, cannot be interpreted in terms of Truth by the mind. That way there lies only contradiction and confusion. The vital lesson which the reader must accept and learn from the Bible, indeed from all scriptures, is that it is a record or divine plan of his or her life. Each and every soul must and will travel the same 'twin' pathways: the descending arc and the ascending arc. As they are the same pathways for all souls, the experiences are the same. Where there are differences in the circumstances of individual souls, this is only because each soul has achieved different levels of consciousness, or arrived at different parts of the pathway. The story of Adam and Eve is therefore the story of the human soul – every human soul. Each aspect of the story holds a particular meaning and is symbolic of a soul experience.

Previously we mentioned the serpent in the tree. The serpent, or serpent power, is traditionally symbolised in Hindu, Vedic and Tantric scriptures as a sleeping serpent coiled around the base of the spine. In these texts it is referred to as 'Kundalini' power. The concept, however, is not limited to Indian scriptures. It is also recorded in the ancient literature of Tibet, Egypt, Sumer, China, Greece and many other cultures and traditions including very early Christianity. Readers may recall that in the Old Testament it is written that Moses raised the serpent high in the wilderness. The pharaohs' head dress reveals a serpent, the feathered serpent of Mexico and South America, all indicative of Kundalini, or the Serpent Power. The word Kundalini comes from ancient Sanskrit, it means 'coiled-up' like a serpent and implies a latent power or great energy ready for sudden release, the basis for the attainment of a higher state of consciousness. Mystics and masters state that it is the fundamental bio-energy of life. Though primarily stored in the sex organs (which is why it is situated at the base of the spine) it is also present throughout the entire body.

Kundalini power is not only an energy or superintelligence present in mystics, gurus and masters, but it is at all times within everyone. In most people, however, it is merely a slow, steady streaming through the body. There are, however, considerable variations in the power, or force, of the streaming. These variations determine the intellectual, psychic, creative and aesthetic development of individuals. The genius and highly sensitive creative artists have a comparatively greater volume of kundalini power streaming through the body and brain. Surrounding and permeating through every cell and molecule this active superintelligence purposefully controls the development of every minute particle of living matter. The stream carries the vital principle of life to every cell, energising, purifying and repairing every life-giving area of the body and brain.

Kundalini is one of seven spiritual centres situated along the cerebro-spinal column called, by some, chakras, and many mystics claim that it is the only link with the Universal Consciousness. The awakening of kundalini, which will only happen after many years of dedicated meditation, is the greatest experience and achievement awaiting the progressing man. How might the kundalini process reveal itself in man? First he is aware of **new** knowledge, the inner meaning and purpose of life. There is a new, higher state of consciousness, the cosmic consciousness of the mystic and the enlightenment of the seer. There also develops an awareness of unity with a higher level of 'knowing'. This is the secret of all spiritual disciplines and esoteric psychologies. It is the key to psychic and healing powers, artistic talents and intellectual creativity. Kundalini achieves all this if correctly aroused with the right spiritual guidance and dedication to meditation.

Certain schools advocate speeding up the flow of kundalini. This can be highly dangerous, painful, destructive and even fatal. The pathway for the kundalini force must be clean, pure and completely free of illusionary contamination, otherwise it intensifies everything that lies in its pathway which could mean a life of seriously deteriorating health and many forms of mental illness.

So, I have attributed to kundalini two basic powers: the power of good and evil, or spiritual and its opposite, thereby establishing, even within kundalini, the law of opposites. Kundalini is the tempter and the spiritual guide. Eve (the soul was tempted by the serpent and because she was unaware of the law of opposites her ignorance was the spark which awakened the senses. The senses created an attachment to the sensual experience. Attachment is the opposite to un-attachment. Un-attachment is All-Spirit. So Eve experienced something that was not purely of the spirit and, therefore, found herself outside the all-perfect state, symbolised by the Garden of Eden. This makes clear the point that truth is knowledge of **all** states that are opposite, love-hate, wisdom-ignorance, beauty-ugliness, spiritual-unspiritual, limitation-infinite, reality-illusion and so on. The Great Intelligence realised that Adam and Eve were not living the 'mature' life. They were ignorant of the **real** and the **unreal**. Therefore to them, at that stage, **all** things were real.

There are many Adams and Eves living with us today. They

are the ignorant who believe everything is real and permanent. The ignorant take everything for granted. They love life and hate death, they cling only to the pleasurable and complain about the painful. The spiritually mature person accepts all pairs of opposites. He has experienced all pairs of opposites. He **knows** that there cannot be good without evil, pleasure without pain, the infinite without the finite, reality without illusion. He has learned the lesson of being dispassionate. Dispassion is neither optimism nor pessimism. He who is always optimistic is a dreamer, but the one who is always pessimistic is negative and inwardly dead. Life is **action** and there can be no action without **reaction**. All our actions are channels for our thoughts and life demands **self-expression**. Without this self-expression and the reaction which follows there is no inner-realisation and, consequently, no meaning of life.

Most individuals can only react. Everything they do, say or think is either compulsive or impulsive. In this way how can they know themselves. The Bhagavad Gita mentions three kinds of ego. The undeveloped has no self-image, no personality, immature, always impulsive and defensive. He only reflects what others think of him. Then there is the sensuous ego. This person has lots of pride and is fascinated by his own image. He is insecure, always trying to prove himself to others. He can also be aggressive because he is always on the defensive. He is never at peace with himself and therefore cannot be at peace with others, His world is hostile and harassing. In contrast to the first two egos there is the mature ego. He is usually quiet, self-effacing, of a humble nature and therefore lives an inconspicuous life.

The spiritually mature person is denoted by his life of harmonious rhythm. The rhythm of action and withdrawal, first contemplation then action, the rhythm of attachment and detachment. This is the rhythm referred to by Zen Buddhists as the Cosmic Rhythm. Without awareness of Cosmic Rhythm there is only conflict, confusion and fear. Cosmic Rhythm is first the recognition, and then the acceptance that there is no level of experience where polarity does not exist. We need to be aware that joy and sadness, pleasure and pain are our finest teachers and that we can find the Way Within just as surely from the evils of life as from the good.

Many perhaps hold the thought that it would be easier to move from the spiritually elated mind through meditation into the realisation of God, but it is a far, far greater achievement to gain full enlightenment on the plane of senses. The mystics have always shown and taught this way which they term the Middle Way for they realised that full enlightenment could never be found unless it is experienced on **every level of consciousness**. The Middle Way of enlightenment is regarded as contrasting with the life of spiritual contemplation, but let us remember that there are certain schools of thought which are so concerned with the Way Within that they tend to neglect here and now. Although this sense world of ours is essentially a world of appearance only and we are, for a while, imprisoned by it, we cannot neglect to ask why it is there. The sense world cannot be other than divine ground, and therefore something of great value must be available to us. It is inevitably a part of the divine plan for us to find out what it is. But for these oppositions in life, and in nature, there would be nothing to inspire the progress of man.

Obviously, what is successfully achieved, or experienced, on the physical level is not of any great importance to the soul. The real values can only be assessed by what has been achieved in the character or personality of the doer. Many men and women have achieved legendary feats in their life; they have established great institutions, created magnificent edifices and awesome works of art, but the actual creations themselves are perishable. First, they are universally appreciated then eventually they become major additions to the world's records, but the **mind** that chooses, first, to create these masterpieces, then inspires the physical effort, courage and determination, these are the imperishable things because they are an inseparable part of the soul, character and personality.

Regrettably, the action and only the action, has become the acceptable pathway of the sense world. The physical completion of the idea is the one goal. The completion, naturally, satisfies a sense demand and once a particular programme has been fulfilled so the decks are cleared to prepare the way for the next programme. This, in turn, will be followed by another. Life has become totally oblivious to a spiritual way, but has developed into a continuous series of projects, with the result that each project becomes an end in itself. Of course, it satisfies a desire perhaps for one or possibly millions of people, but each project, knowingly or unknowingly, becomes the end. In other words, each plan, project or programme, no matter how gigantic or magnificent, is of the same material as a beefburger. Its purpose is the same, a desire has been satisfied. A. C. Benson, in his book, **Escape and other Essays**, obviously came to the same conclusion when he wrote,

> 'Satisfied desire is the least contented of moods . . . This strange sense of escape which drives us into activity and energy seems given us not that we may realise our aims, which turn out hollow and vapid enough, when they are realised, but that we may drink deep of the experience for the sake of its beneficent effect upon us.'

He goes on to say that the work we do matters very little to the soul, but the fact that we are engaged in some work brings satisfaction to the senses. This piece of wisdom will give little satisfaction to those who are striving for better societies, better living standards, radical social reforms or establishing peace on earth. Of course, these are spiritual motives but what matters most of all are the **solutions** to these problems – and **permanent** solutions. If we begin with programmes and plans, no permanent solutions will be found in these because all programmes and plans are goals and ends. Solutions are to be looked for in the **spiritual minds** of which the material consciousness is the **means** by which the programmes become solutions. Solutions are to be found initially in the realm of spiritual consciousness and not first in programmes.

There are many who will disagree with this way of action, but let us pause to consider. If a hungry man is given several beefburgers, a new suit of clothes, a warm, comfortable place to rest, sufficient work to keep him occupied and to earn money what, exactly, have you achieved? For the moment he is no longer hungry, he has a warm suit and place to sleep. But is that enough? You have provided, perhaps, ample material comforts but is that the permanent solution? The only certain goodness is in what **you** have done. Your actions may create a sense of gratitude, even a feeling of kindliness within the receiver but is it enough? How long can you go on giving? Satisfaction and gratitude may be expressed but how are they to be sustained? You can devote your entire life to giving to this person but how much are you really helping him? What happens if you suddenly die? It is always possible that your example will change the attitude of the receiver. Your kindness may set him on the road to spiritual understanding, but will it happen in every case? It is unlikely. So, where does the permanent solution lie? Happiness is never to be found in an abundance of things, but only in the consciousness. No one can command happiness in another, or can create happiness by satisfying their demands. So a deeper analysis of social reforms and world plans are called for. Clearly, we cannot begin with plans on the outside, so we must begin on the inside – the consciousness, or mind. We have already stated that all conflicts begin in the mind because man's thoughts and ideals are centralised upon the sensual fruits of his actions. Permanent happiness will never be found in this jungle of sensual demands.

The obvious fact is, of course, that with all the problems, conflicts and disharmonious elements of life totally removed, leaving nothing but the soul of man, it is very difficult to see how the soul can progress. What should it progress to and from **what** should it progress? It is equally obvious that souls are manifesting on differing levels of consciousness. We live amongst saints and sinners and if the spiritual essence of the soul is of the same infinite quality, then clearly some souls have progressed and others have still some way to go. In other words, some of the baser elements of life have been eliminated.

Therefore, something of great value is potentially available through a **way of action** in this sense world of ours.

All action is the working out on the material level of our inner self. Our choice of action is prompted by our desires. As every action must create a **reaction** which we experience, for better or worse, therefore every reaction teaches us something about the **quality** of the desire. So it is the way of action which allows us to experience a 'clash of opposites' without which every soul would be held fast in a state of motiveless, motionless stagnation.

It is, therefore, of great importance that every soul should strive with all effort to eliminate the baser elements of our consciousness once they have been recognised by the reaction. A person may act through greed, selfishness and cruelty, and this person will experience many conflicts and disharmonies, but the person who acts through love, tolerance and understanding is not caught up in the world of ego-action. As Buddha points out, the majority of people act because they wish to enjoy sensual pleasure for themselves. He also pointed out that it was the 'fruits' of the action which were the main attraction. This person blames everything and everyone for his misfortunes and never realises that the reason for these lie within himself.

In contrast, the enlightened person accepts all pairs of opposites because he realises that he will never know goodness unless he experiences evil; pleasure needs pain and life requires death. Therefore, as we have seen, the spiritual way ahead through action requires constant discipline on the material level. As Buddha said, it involves the renunciation of the 'fruits' of the action. It also demands a dispassionate attitude to success and failure. Dispassion is neither optimistic nor is it pessimistic. To be always optimistic is to be a dreamer. On the other hand, to be always pessimistic is to be negative and morbid. Dispassion is the middle way between the negative and the positive. It is being involved in action but remaining unattached to the reaction. Dispassion is the natural rhythm of nature which can only be experienced and achieved through normal daily action. All life is action and there can be no action without tension. Tension is only possible when the mind is attracted away from the middle way and becomes entangled with the negative. All our actions are merely channels for self-expression and every moment of our conscious life-demands self-expression. If it were possible not to have self-expressions, then the soul would receive no experiences, therefore no 'nourishment' and consequently there would be no meaning to anything or to life. Our self-expression should be used as a form of guidelines which would indicate when we are veering off to the negative or too much to the optimistic, the realm of the dreamer. The dispassionate person exercises total control of the inner self. Most people can only react. Their self-expressions are either compulsive or impulsive, defensive or aggressive. They have not achieved the natural rhythm of the inner self, they have not found the middle way. Their actions or responses are enslaved by the ego-mind. They are not free to be creative or expressive. All creative or expressive responses are free from inner restraints.

Therefore, the watchword for creative, balanced living is **middle-way**. Nothing happens to us by chance or accident. We create everything that happens to us. We experience what we create ourselves. We make and guide our destiny by our own actions and we enjoy or suffer according to the quality of our reactions. We earn our peace or pain. No one has the power to give us peace or pain unless we first give **them** the power. For the escapists or opportunists there is no peace. Zen teaches us that peace can only be found on the middle-way, but, perhaps MacNeile Dixon in his stimulating book, **The Human Situation** put it simply and clearly when he wrote:

> 'This clash of opposites may have brought it about that we have a Universe at all, and we ourselves, its offsprings, are in being, that from this dark soil (the earth plane) of conflict creation sprang. But for these oppositions in nature and human life (the world wide warfare of the Eternal Two) nothing would have taken place, all would be sunk in a motiveless and motionless stagnation.'

CHAPTER EIGHT

THE LAW OF KARMA

Life Becomes What Man Does

Karma is the ultimate law of the universe, the source, origin and fount of all other laws which exist throughout Nature. It is the unerring law which adjusts effect to cause on the physical, mental and spiritual planes of being. As no cause remains without its due effect from greatest to least, from a cosmic disturbance down to the movement of your hand, and as like produces like, karma is that unseen and unknown law which adjusts wisely, intelligently and equitably each effect to cause, tracing the latter back to its producer.

There is hardly a part of our universe which is not experiencing war, disaster, revolution, terrorism, starvation or plague. All over the world millions of people are praying for peace hoping that the many unfortunate incidents will be resolved. And perhaps as many people are also asking the question, why does God allow this, or why does God not put an end to these problems? Others with a little knowledge of esoteric truths simply dismiss these tragedies as, 'Karma'. To many of these people Karma is a mechanical, soulless thing, a retributive action attributed to some mystical cause in which, very often, innocent souls are involved. Others think of it as nothing more than a simple credit and debit account, jealously watched over by some cosmic overlord. The fundamental truths behind the purpose and the way of Karma cannot possibly be explained on the intellectual level. The intellect deals exclusively with facts arising from our sensual or phenomenal world. Though the sandy beaches and the deserts of our world are vast and numerous, the number of grains of sand and pebbles comprising the beaches and deserts are not infinite. They are numbered because these areas and the particles contained therein are finite. Of all the spiritual laws Karma is the ultimate and infinite force, but still a living, intelligent and compassionate law.

In the previous chapter we gave much thought to that which we called the 'middle-way'. Life for everyone, be he beggar or king, a fool or a sage, is on a pilgrimage of slow enlightenment. The middle-way of learning is through the experience of opposites. Every experience, every emotion, always creates its opposite. Wars and conflicts, both on universal and individual levels, are created and will continue to be created as long as man fails to recognise the doctrine of Karma and the nature of the law of opposites.

Only by experience after experience and by constant observation can we hope to achieve the meanest vision of these doctrines, which are ultimate and all-embracing laws. Though Karma is the least understood and the most neglected truth in the western world, this serious omission is emphatically of man's own choosing. For many years, perhaps for many lives, man has built up a totally false idea of his true identity. It is the most difficult thing for the man of the Western world to believe that the character which he is and which he believes to be the real self is in fact an illusion. He would find it even more difficult to accept that this character, which he alone has built up, is the sole cause of all his fears and sufferings. Therefore it follows that only he who observes and studies the way of Karma, accepting without question or using any form of excuse, the action and reaction of Karma, will surely find freedom from the lower self and its constant, insatiable demands for the sensual things of the world.

It is probably true that some readers have already reacted to the references to Karma. This is probably because the word suggests something of the mystique of Eastern cultures and is, therefore, best left to the mystics. Other readers of a more religiously inclined nature may feel antagonistic as though some strange foreign doctrine is being forced upon them.

Karma is a Sanskrit word and when translated simply means **action**. Every soul is committed to some form of action every day simply to fulfil some purpose. In other words, there is a positive reason behind every action and the reason is to achieve an **effect** which we hope will benefit us in some way. Therefore **reason** of the mind is the **cause**, and the **benefit** we hope to achieve is the **effect**. Therefore, Karma is simply the law of **cause** and **effect**. But, as we have learned from experience, not all causes are beneficial. They can be painful. So he who puts the cause into action will suffer or enjoy the effect.

Karma, the ultimate, unseen law, is taught in every scripture throughout the world and is a cardinal belief of the Christian fathers because as St. Paul preached, 'God is not mocked, for whatsoever a man soweth so shall he also reap', indicating, quite clearly that this particular law wisely and unmistakably traces each cause back to its producer. Karma, itself, creates nothing. It cannot design experiences of pain or happiness. It is man or more accurately, the mind of man which creates the causes **and** karma (effects). The law simply enhances the harmony, when the cause is of a harmonious mind, or ruthlessly re-adjusts the effects for the purpose of re-establishing the inner (also universal) harmony. And these re-adjustments will continue until the mind acknowledges the nature of the cause or the state of disharmony.

Karma is the product of man's own thought and the effects which unerringly return are simply a reflection of the quality of the thought behind the action. The most famous verse in the **Dhammapada** puts this point forward very clearly,

> *All that we are is the result of what we have thought:*
> *It is founded on our thoughts, it is made up of our thoughts.*

No matter how far we go back in history we will find that man has interminably fought for his freedom or the restoration of some 'right'. No matter how often or how long he has fought his battles to achieve some environmental change that would restore his 'right' or achieve a satisfaction, the vital **essence** of his cause has always escaped him. This is because the **causes** for his freedom and his addiction to his 'rights' are only within his mind. In other words, the solutions must be found in the mind and not on the outside of him. Therefore, until the nature of these causes are analysed and understood in terms of reality and removed from the mind, the desire to achieve the effects on the outside will always remain. These patterns of thought, the desires and the inevitable actions which are prompted, constitute a kind of bondage. The disturbing consequences which follow are natural attempts by Karmic law to restore the lost harmony. Unfortunately, man never recognises these as spiritual efforts on the part of Karma but only as lost chances, bad luck or accidents.

And so it follows that every thought, desire and action inescapably produces consequences which may be pleasant, sad or extremely painful. The consequences may follow quickly or be delayed by hours, days, months and even years. Let us take one example. A person takes a drink of alcohol to relieve a moment of tension, or fear. This constitutes but a few moments of escape. The unfortunate result is that every time that same distressed state of mind returns a part of the mind will remind that person that relief can be obtained by taking alcohol. The final result could be that within months or years that person, having become dependent upon alcohol to deal with a difficult recurring situation, could become an alcoholic. To be an alcoholic is a serious, degrading condition of mind which may, in the end, prove fatal, therefore, proving that Karmic consequences have taken some months or years to be effective. Another example, where the effects, or consequences, would take effect immediately, is if a person took a deadly poison.

It is, then, what we **are** that creates for us the circumstances of our existence. And what we are means the quality or pattern of our mind. To simplify this particular truth let us think of the mind as comprising a series of innumerable, intricate patterns where each item represents an action of both good and evil. Each of these items we have created some time in the past. Which means, in effect, there is no fate, destiny or event which we have not made and do make for ourselves. As it is written in the **Bhagavad Gita**, 'We are today the product of our long past and we shall be tomorrow what we have made of ourselves today'. In other words, we are a slave to that which we created yesterday, but remain the master of our future.

Many people feel antipathetic towards the idea of Karma because they believe it is a cruel and unforgiving law. They think of it as a kind of remorseless machine which makes them suffer for something of which they are totally ignorant or, indeed, cannot even remember. We must remind the reader, that Karma is incapable of creating or designing anything. Suffering is the result of Karmic action being attracted to those areas of ignorance or evil for the sole purpose of **re-adjusting** the cosmic harmony. Karma did not create the areas of ignorance or evil, man himself did that. For example, consider the phenomenon of fire. If man is completely ignorant of the nature of fire and never in his existence has he seen or experienced fire, then should he, because of his ignorance, plunge his hand into a fire the instant pain that follows will immediately apply the correct effects which will not only teach him that it is dangerous to touch fire, but also the area of ignorance will be instantly transformed into wisdom.

Within the soul pattern of every man there are areas of ignorance or unknowing, and Karmic law, the spiritual dynamic effect of **causes**, is directed to transform areas of 'unknowing' and awaken them into areas of wisdom or 'knowing'. This is the Universal Law's way of helping man to 'know thyself'. Meaning not only to know the good within, but more important, to recognise the evil and ignorance within. This is the only way to total freedom from suffering, to peace of soul – to Nirvana.

This fundamental law, the only and vital basis for the attainment of the infinite, undying self must be thoroughly experienced and accepted both from the negative and positive aspect before the law of Karma can be completely understood and recognised for its purpose. Whilst love remains the supreme reigning power in the universe, its presence being felt on every significant level of consciousness, there must exist a governing law on each level; therefore as Karma is subject to the supreme power of love, it cannot be considered that Karma impresses a cold, impersonal influence upon the universe.

There are many seemingly useless and extremely tragic incidents in life. We observe brilliant, young artists suddenly struck blind, young children involved in serious and sometimes fatal accidents, uniquely gifted persons rendered helpless in the prime of their life by some disease; incidents which we casually pass off as unfortunate accidents or moments of bad luck. Many find it difficult to accept these poignant happenings as a vital part of the philosophy of life. In the face of such immensely challenging events, it is little wonder that so many minds are filled or overcome by doubt.

Is it true or false? Is the universe cosmos or chaos? Whatever the answer there is one thing for sure, this planet cannot be **partly** ruled by immutable law and **partly** by chance. Either the law exists or it exists not at all. If it does exist then he is a fool who does not acclaim it far and wide and consider it when regarding the smallest detail of his daily life, or recognise it as the highest creative intelligence which constitutes the universe. There is absolutely no evidence at all for assuming that man's mind is the highest result of the planet's evolutionary process. For example, consider the countless millions of species of animal and insect which represent an inventive ingenuity of the highest possible order. How can this be remotely considered as something sometimes cosmic and at other times chaotic. There can only be one answer and that answer is brilliantly provided by Edward Carpenter in his book, **The Art of Creation** which says, 'Creation is a stupendous and perpetually renewed work of art, and everlasting evolution and expression on inner meanings into outward forms, not only in the great whole, but in every tiniest part.'

Therefore, it must be accepted that the laws of intelligence which make up the universe are of infinite variety and of infinite degrees of development. Yet all of them must have a common object of existence, a common co-ordinating intelligence. Such a law or intelligence can be understood, not by the logical mind of man, but only by a deep spiritual understanding.

But let us return to the so-called unmerited suffering of **innocents**. Do they deserve all that happens to them or are there just occasional accidents in which they suffer without justice? It should first be remembered, and considered, that many incidents enter into our life by avenues which are unforeseeable and not all of them are pleasant. These incidents cover every kind of experience from those we most enjoy and those which we fear. Let us now consider several possibilities.

1. Is it possible to consider a world which has been regarded by MacNeile Dixon in his book, **The Human Situation?** That but for the oppositions in nature and human life (the worldwide warfare of the eternal two) nothing would have taken place, all would be sunk in a motiveless, motionless stagnation', or, the world referred to by Keats as, 'a vale of soul-making', and then to consider a world where there are only possibilities for good without any possibilities for badness or evil, without adversities from where would we receive the opportunities to move forward and achieve better things? We must not lose sight of these when we are faced by tragic events.

2. Are there incidents the cause of which are beyond the intelligence of man, and causes so remote that there are no possible ways of tracing them?

3. If we could see precisely and unerringly all the details of the laws of nature and the **entire** pattern of circumstances on the material side at any given moment, then and only then, is it possible for us to calculate any and every situation in the universe and so rearrange things beforehand.

If all this were possible, then we would have the power to remove the vital influnces of the 'clash of opposites' which, according to the great masters, brought the universe about, when we, ourselves, were brought into being. The 'vale of soul-making' would not exist and the possibility is that all would be sunk in motiveless, motionless stagnation. The reader should seriously consider the meaning of progress, or the manifestation of the soul. Is it not the overcoming of all that lies beneath the attaining all that which is in being above?

Fortunately for the human race, it is not possible for any mortal to know all the details of all the laws, so there exists the 'saving' source of **unpredictability**. Considering the infinite number and continuous happenings, or acts, influencing a particular soul, we must assume that total predictability is impossible. This analysis, though totally inadequate, should help us to realise that for the divine, infinite, or cosmic mind from which **all** actions originate, there exists no possibility of chance or accident, but we must recognise the fallibility of the **undeveloped finite mind** and therefore accept the existence of chance or accident.

The finite mind is a compendium of all past experiences during its long association with matter. Therefore, except for the occasional flash of intuition, which is the experience of few people, the finite mind, continuously occupied with its daily existence, cannot be expected to foresee or predict on the basis of its own past experiences. The tragic 'accidents' with which we are concerned are not solely the results of material or physical causes, they also result from emotional and mental factors. Forgetfulness, carelessness, lack of attention, inefficiency and, very often, greed (providing inadequate or poor quality services, means and material) are the motivating factors.

So now we can, I hope, begin to see that an individual soul, or a group of connected souls, cannot possibly be in a position to be aware of the incalculable causes precipitated not only by the individual, but the many other souls involved. All Karmic action of a disturbing nature has its operational mechanism on the level of **mind** and it is what we **are** on this mental level which automatically and unerringly attracts to us not only the circumstances, but also the **reaction** to our response to the circumstances. Therefore, according to the philosopher Loftus Hare in **Mysticism of East and West** 'Man becomes what he does.' On this basis there can be no such thing as chance or accident but only the immutable law of cause and effect operating through the individual mind and the group mind.

As revealed to Jacob in his dream of the many souls standing on the ladder ascending from earth to heaven, man has many levels of cognition. Each step on the stairway is a higher level of spiritual awareness. Through each level the evolving man must climb until he finds and becomes the infinite level of consciousness which, only then, will he learn he has always been.

Meanwhile, on the lower levels of the intellect, where doubts constantly arise and cloud the truths of man's purpose, Karmic law can only be considered as a just law which patiently, wisely and intelligently applies each effect to its cause so that the thinker, or producer, can be rightly adjusted on the physical, mental and spiritual planes of his being and thus, little by little, or act by act, guided back to his true purpose.

Karma is not a blind or unconscious law. Not only does it dominate all other natural laws, but it is living and intelligent as are all other guiding laws in the universe. Like the great masters who work from the centre to the outer, as opposed to the unenlightened man who works from the outer to the outer, Karma works from the infinite centre through **all** levels to the physical. Another law fundamentally involved to secure the continued progression of man's soul is the law of the 'pair of opposites' which means **Spirit** and **matter, subject** and **object**. From the constant interplay of this original duality arises the motive, acts and reactions and, therefore, the Karma which we, ourselves, create and suffer until the nature of the motive is recognised as illusion.

Another vital principle is the 'cycle of becoming', which implies the necessary pilgrimage of every soul originating from the pure spirit into densest matter, after which it undertakes the return path back to pure spirit. This gigantic cycle of transformation is not solely confined to the soul of man but is within every living element within the earth. These infinite cycles of birth, death and re-birth are to be observed in the atom, vegetation and animal.

Why and what is man in this awesome scheme of things? I

must begin by reminding the reader that man **is** essentially and eternally pure spirit. He is of that absolute state which is beyond the reach and analysis of thought. For the purpose of simplicity we can say that man is 'clothed' in many layers of veils, each layer as it reaches outwards gradually increasing in density. Each layer may be described as a vehicle which enables him to 'become' (for a while) and communicate with the descending planes of consciousness. Each vehicle is a kind of super-fine fabric or matter, the lowest of which is of our earth material, and the highest of which is of such fineness that it virtually does not exist. Nonetheless, each layer from the densest to the finest is of an impermanent nature. As Karma inexorably and unerringly adjusts the effects, thereby increasing the universal harmony, the lower level of consciousness changes as the outer 'veil' dissolves.

Certain schools of meditation refer to the 'veils' as skins like those associated with an onion. Through the practice of meditation the student is instructed first to repeat over and over again all the things he is **not**. For example, 'I am not this mind: I am not this body: I am not something that dies' and so on. With deep establishment of the realisation that he is not these things, the outer layers of skins dissolve.

Blavatsky wrote in the **Secret Doctrine**, 'The only decree (command) of Karma, an eternal and immutable decree, is absolute harmony in the world of matter as in the world of spirit. It is not, therefore, Karma that rewards or punishes, but it is we who reward and punish ourselves, according as we work with and through nature, abiding by the laws on which the harmony depends, or breaking them.'

Man, as spirit, or the highest form of self-consciousness rules the universe with the help of Karma, his beneficent companion. But once he has created Karma he must then bow the knee to the monster of his creation, and it will not be for him to complain that fate or destiny has against his will frustrated his actions or committed him to an unjust reaction. In other words, the law of Karma is completely impersonal. It is the helpful and obedient servant of its creator – **man**. It is not the obedient slave of an avenging god. Thus it is logical to assume that it is of no value to attempt to placate it, pray to it, condemn it or argue with it because Karma is the product of our own thought.

Certainly, there are gross inequalities in life. Many people are severely handicapped from the very beginning, with deformed bodies, blindness and other impediments. For others the environment is of squalor and ugliness or, perhaps, made intolerably cruel by indifferent, uncaring parents. If these conditions are not by chance and are not planned by God, what explanation exists that carries sufficient assurance that all are born equal and that we live in a **just** world? If we take our stand on the side of those who believe that each soul born into the world is a **new** creation, then we would have no alternative but to accept that man is no more than a pawn on the chessboard of life, moved by some unseen hand without compassion or plan; he can be likened to some blown leaf on the winds of a pointless destiny.

In our attempt to put forward an acceptable philosophy of life, one which **proves** God is just, good and all-loving to every soul, and to show there is clear meaning to life, in spite of the gross inequalities, we cannot ignore the timeless beliefs set down by the ancient sages of the East. Our first step is to reject the belief that each soul born into the Earth is in some inexplicable way a **new** creation of God. Plato believed strongly that the soul was immortal and this, obviously, implies an **infinite** future, and therefore it must imply an infinite past. Then, again in the **Phaedo** Plato states that if souls only come into existence at birth, then their survival of death would be an impossibility.

Belief in the pre-existence of the soul is supported by the doctrines of re-incarnation originating with the ancient sages of India. It is prominently recorded in the doctrines of both Buddhism and Hinduism. Among the early Greeks it was taught in the schools of Empedocles, Pythagoras and Plato. It also appears in the teachings of Philo of Alexandria. In early Roman times it was accepted by Cicero and Seneca. The Druids of Gaul also embraced the doctrines of pre-existence. In more recent times it was accepted by Giordano Bruno, Swedenborg, Goethe, Lichtenberg, Hume, Schopenhauer and many other great minds of ancient and modern philosophy. The names of these great scholars are sufficient to show that the doctrines of pre-existence has commended itself to some of the greatest and most learned minds in history.

But let us, at this point, put our own mind to work. Let us appeal to our own senses of logic and reason. Consider, first, the vast area of separation between the most spiritual and the wisest persons we know and the cruel, degenerate wretch. Now, think of the masters, saints, mystics and sages and compare their minds with the lowly, unspiritual monsters history has recorded and others we have encountered. The average life-span of a human being is approximately eighty years. Could it be possible that such a gigantic difference of achievement and failure could be reached in such a short space of time? Now consider the great standards of the legendary maestros, poets, writers and philosophers and that of the ordinary man in the street. Surely, the incredible difference between the two cannot be accountable in terms of a few score years? Surely, it would be wiser to accept that the differences are the result of **lives** of past achievements.

To further the above considerations, let us not forget about the appearance on Earth, from time to time, of the child prodigies. For example, Sir William Hamilton thoroughly mastered Hebrew at the age of three. At the age of thirteen he had acquired considerable knowledge of at least thirteen languages. Among these, besides the classical and modern European languages, were included Persian, Arabic, Sanskrit, Hindustani and even Malay. At the age of fourteen he wrote a letter to the Persian ambassador. In reply the ambassador said that he did not think that there was a man in Britain who could have written such a document in Persian. Brinkley (President, Astronomer Royal of Ireland) said of Hamilton when eighteen, 'This boy is the first mathematician of the age.' Throughout the ages there have been many remarkable geniuses who demonstrated rare gifts before they even attended school. Genius in children cannot be ignored because there is no explanation.

There must be an explanation, there must be a cause. Plato recognised this and in his view, 'The knowledge which is acquired early and easily is "old" knowledge and represents an overflow into the present life of great achievements gained in the past life.' For example, Mozart and Chopin were both composing classical symphonies and playing an instrument with outstanding skill at an extremely early age.

If the case for pre-existence is a strong one, and many of the most outstanding philosophers and mystics believed that it is, then the question of inequalities, accidents and a life of chance presents no difficulties, because whatever a soul has achieved before, there is no reason why it cannot do it again and again.

Thousands of deep thinkers and most gifted poets have seen, with absolute certainty, the truth of Karmic law which orthodox religion has expelled in favour of certain rigid creeds and dogmas which the original founders would know nothing about.

In his remarkable book, **Reincarnation**, E. D. Walker, a scholar of pre-existence, says

> 'Once the whole civilised world embraced reincarnation, and found therein the complete answer to the riddle of man's descent and destiny. But the western branch of the race, in working out the material conquests of the world, has acquired the compensating discontent of a material philosophy. It has lost the old faith and drifted into a shadowy region, where the eagerness for "practical" things rejects whatever cannot be physically proven.'

The East has accepted the law since time immemorial. The West accepted it for a long time after the birth of Christianity; Greek, Roman, Egyptian and Jew accepted the law. The Bible shows its prevalence in the days of Jesus and the Master's adoption of the law without question. On Karma the Master said, 'By their fruits shall you know them . . . every **good** tree bringest forth **good** fruit, but the corrupt tree bringeth forth evil fruit. A good tree cannot bring forth evil fruit, neither can a corrupt tree bring forth good fruit.' And he who rewards accordingly is no **being**, however great, but the Father within, the Buddha within, the **self** within from which has evolved both man and the all-embracing law.

When questioned about pre-existence, Jesus said, when asked about the person who was born blind, 'It was neither he who has sinned nor his parents.' Clearly it was he in a previous life.

Man and the law of Karma can be thought of as the same reality, with man as the administrator of the law which in a sense he actually is. Life necessarily is a pilgrimage of slow development, a middle-way through birth after birth, always learning through experience after experience, until the self, the God within has once more gained total mastery.

CHAPTER NINE

WHAT IS THE SELF?

The newcomer to esoteric philosophy may be excused for being confused by the many different expressions used by teachers, philosophers and adepts concerning various scriptures. The reader strives to grasp the meaning of difficult metaphysical expressions with the earnest hope that he may understand something of the true structure of the real self.

There are those who speak of 'veils' which stand between the less real and the absolute real. Others refer to the structure as resembling the 'skins' of the onion. Indian philosophers mention 'Maya', that which reduced the light so that we live in a twilight world. Though not totally unreal, it is the furthest removed from the absolute real. Teachers of the Western world simply describe the structure as 'the many levels of consciousness.' Jesus expressed the view, concerning the structure as, 'In my Father's house there are many mansions.' Meaning, of course, that the structure of self comprises many levels of consciousness. It is clear that all of these teachers were trying to express difficult metaphysical views in order to convey some idea concerning the structure of the real self.

What then are these veils or skins which separate the true self from the lower self, or earth-conscious mind? Why are they there? What is their real purpose and from where do they originate? Why is it necessary for veil after denser veil to enshroud the essential spirit until all thoughts and awareness are concentrated on a world which (according to mystics) is likened to a sombre twilight when compared to the brilliance of the spirit of man?

The Hindu view is that the objective world really exists. It is not an illusion but that which is simply the furthest away from the absolute reality. It is also their thought, that, though the world of phenomena must not be regarded as the ultimate real, in being a form of life it is an expression of the ultimate real, therefore still to be considered divine.

Radhakrishnan tells us that on the first levels of real, or mystical, consciousness is the Intuitive Self; but behind this level there are infinite depths of the Essential Self which also serve as extremely fine veils between the Intuitive Self and the Infinite, Absolute Centre or Essence. Of this Essence the great mystics of the East tell us that it is the **true** being of man. The real 'I' which is immortal and divine. The ego-mind, or lower self, can be considered, as far as we know, the densest of the veils because it is closely and always associated with matter. This is the mind which ordinary, unenlightened beings believe themselves to be and with which they associate themselves.

It is possible, after long practice of meditation, for the ego to experience the briefest glimpse of the higher self. This is known as a mystical experience and one which is so overwhelming and extraordinary that no language can fully describe it. For further explanations of this experience the reader should, once again, refer to the introduction. The divine purpose and essential meaning of life is that the ego shall be totally absorbed into the highest self, but this can only come about when the final veil has gone, or the last 'skin' has dropped away. It was in referring to this truth that Buddha said, 'In no-thing shall you find the truth.' Because he, like all masters and mystics, knew that only attachment to the things of the world created and kept in being the many layers of veils. Total absorption of all the veils is called, **'Samadhi'** by Indian sages. He who experiences **Samadhi** becomes a completely changed person because the ego-self no longer exists. Should the reader at this point become somewhat apprehensive, or be concerned regarding his personal identity, thinking, perhaps, that he is destined to be absorbed into some limitless consciousness, devoid of the sense of 'being', this is not the case. There is always complete, serene unity with the **one**.

Though the sense of the essential ego remains, there is no 'egoism' because the ego becomes the complete servant of the Higher Self, whereas in the past the ego-self was complete master of all the senses. The senses are the centres of desire and the sources of attachment to sense objects.

Radhakrishnan describes this situation in the following way:

> 'The conscious division and separation from the Divine Being (the object from the subject) which is the normal condition of un-regenerated (unenlightened) humanity is broken down. Man becomes what he beholds (total freedom). The distinction between the object and the subject is absorbed by it (the Divine Being), comprehending nothing in particular, holding itself in nothingness (non-attachment), the soul finds itself as having ALL. A strange quietness enters the soul a great peace enters its being, the Vision, the Spark (enlightenment), the supreme movement of unification, or, conscious realisation, sets the whole being ablaze with perfect purpose. The supreme awareness, the ultimate felt presence, brings with it a rapture beyond joy, a knowledge beyond reason, a sensation more intense than that of life itself, infinite in peace and harmony'.

This is the experience which awaits the man who wakes up from his hitherto accepted way of living. The experience can be compared to a person who has lived a long nightmare of dreams which were always elusive, never satisfying, always frightening, and the awakening to a beautiful, bright spring morning, finding himself free from all worries, cares and responsibilities. All dreamers, when dreaming, experience what they believe at the time, to be real. Once awake the dream is seen to be an illusion and the awakened state becomes the reality. For many the world of objects and things, for a while, appears to be the real world. This is because of the numerous veils which successfully screen the real, or absolute, state. That which we cannot see, touch, or become conscious of creates within us a state of total ignorance, with the result that that which we see, touch and experience becomes the reality. We cannot search for, ask ourselves, or question, 'What are these veils which obscure the rest of me?', because to our normal state of consciousness they do not exist. It is this state of ignorance, or earth attachment, which make us rely more and more upon the ego-mind. It is the only thing we recognise and, seemingly, can depend upon for our existence. Just as the dreamer forgets the 'self' of the normal waking state, so the man attached to the ego state (the world of clashing opposites, good and evil, wisdom and ignorance, joy and pain) remains as ignorant of his true spiritual identity as the dreamer in sleep.

In spite of the many dense veils surrounding the infinite levels of consciousness, every veil from the densest to the finest is sustained by the absolute level of super-consciousness, meaning, of course, at no place or time is it possible for the Divine Self to be absent or separated from the 'whole-being', physical, mental and spiritual. When we look sufficiently deep into the actions of man, intuitively, psychically and esoterically we cannot help but realise that **all** of man's actions are motivated by his unceasing search for happiness, contentment, security and freedom from fear and want. Man, in truth, has little idea where to find real happiness so he plunges again and again into the only world he is aware of – the world of opposites. He finds happiness but he fails to find permanent happiness. But, ever hopeful, he returns again and again to his accepted world of attachment. The fundamental difference between partial and permanent happiness is that the former searches outwardly and the latter inwardly.

Clearly, the next problem is how do we find the way **in** and how do we learn to dissolve the many obscuring veils. First, we must achieve the total realisation that the ego, with which we have always and naturally identified ourselves, is not the real self. In other words, we must **know** that there **is** another and higher self and it is an inseparable part of ourselves. Secondly, we must realise fully that the ego-self cannot possibly understand or realise the supreme self. The ego-self can only concern itself with knowledge and information of the outer. The

Supreme Consciousness cannot possibly be an object of knowledge.

So, how do we find the way in? Clearly, considering what has already been said, the ego cannot find a way in. The truth is that the ego can do nothing. However, we must realise the ego **does** exist, but it does not exist in the **eternal** sense. This is, by its very nature it was destined to exist in a temporal state. In other words, it is not **real**. The Divine Self is infinite and eternal whereas the ego is temporarily absorbed in the life of the soul and only for a time thinking of itself as real. In spite of this, its temporal appearance must be for a purpose. Somehow, somewhere the ego factor fits into the cosmic plan. Therefore, there must be some benefit, some gain to the soul. We must never assume that there are things which exist and nothing is to be gained by their appearance, no matter how brief. Everything is an essential part of the cosmic plan and there is meaning in everything including the temporal, and our purpose is to find out what it is.

In spite of all that has been said about self, ego and the temporal states the very fact that **something** exists, even temporarily, means it must represent a quality of consciousness which **could** indicate some starting point. The conclusion from this is that the ego is a **means** of ultimately achieving that something higher when the ego eventually dissolves.

Obviously it is the wisdom of the Higher Self which prompts and patiently guides the ego along a particular path which will finally fulfil its purpose before its absorption. This surely reveals how blind and mistaken the narrow sectarian organisations are who have no esoteric or mystical insight whatsoever. There can never be a mass, or collective, move forward because each individual soul progresses according to its temperament and spiritual growth.

To return to the question; what is this benefit which can be achieved through the ego's association with the material world, at the same time, realising that the ego itself cannot achieve reality? This statement may confuse many readers and may even bring about a sense of hopelessness and bewilderment. They are confronted by the ego-self day after day. In every action, every thought it is there, strong and dominant. Yet to be told by every teacher, mystic and sage that it cannot achieve reality or truth, which is the only way to freedom and peace, is like asking the student to understand the impossible. At the same time to assume that the temporal self can achieve nothing is to render the whole process of temporality useless, meaningless and unnecessary. If this can be the truth then what of the law of opposites? We are told that the positive needs the negative aspect to gain significance and identity. Reality needs illusion and so on. On this basis we must assume that the eternal needs the temporal. Therefore, temporality must be a truth with a purpose. What that purpose is we must find out.

Let us begin by accepting that the ego-self does not exist in the **eternal** sense. But the fact that it exists at all surely indicates that even in its temporal state it must be some kind of **starting point** for some profounder level of consciousness of which at our present level of consciousness we have no concept whatsoever. The next fact we must consider is even though the ego is in being for only a limited time it **is** in existence and all existence **is** life. From this we **must** assume that some part, or aspect, of the Higher Self, for a time, is immersed in, and lives through, the ego's time of existence. Therefore, there must be some purpose, some gain or benefit to be achieved from this temporal being before it is finally absorbed by the Higher Self.

Could the starting point be found in the situation of attachment? The ego, we know is only kept in being by its attachment to the phenomenal or sensual world. Could it be that all the ego's strivings, seeking and aspirations are, in truth, expressions of the deep-lying Higher Self for the purpose of leading us to the meaning and eventual realisation of **detachment**? Throughout this book I have stressed, in many ways, the vital importance of the Law of Opposites. By now we should not have doubted that the Law of Opposites, in fact all laws, are truths designed to lead us through the maze of illusion and ignorance to freedom. I have always upheld that Jesus was much more than a man, he was a truth that symbolised **all** men and their eternal struggles. Like **all** men Jesus experienced fear, anger and pain. There are some who say he also experienced loss of faith. They are relating to the time when Jesus, hung on the cross, cried out in fear, 'Father, Father, why hast thou forsaken me'? True, it is a curious cry for a Master to make. But then he also said, 'No one comes unto the Father except by me.' Meaning that **his** way of life, **his** experiences were **everyman's** experiences. Then again, he said, 'No one comes unto the Father except by way of the cross.' Clearly the cross is symbolic of pain, suffering, crucifixion by an adopted material way of life, and finally the sacrificing of these ways. Jesus was a leader of men and like all leaders he must first go ahead, experiencing testing and searching out the difficult ways ahead.

Therefore, we can conclude that the starting point is the experience of attachment, revealing to us that attachment means pain, suffering and crucifixion, but finally leads us to freedom and **de-tachment**. In the Christian scriptures we find considerable reference to de-tachment. For example, 'Seek ye first the Kingdom of God and His righteousness,' and, 'Lay not up for yourself treasures upon earth where moth and rust doth corrupt.' When Jesus cried out from the cross he did not express a loss of faith, but simply demonstrated a necessary act of freedom which all men must undergo. The cry of fear came not from the Higher Self, but from the lower, or ego-self, which felt its power now rapidly dropping away as the Absolute Spirit absorbed it. This is made clear by a statement which immediately followed His cry of fear, 'It is finished. Unto Thee I commend my Spirit.' This is the complete de-tachment, or supreme sacrifice.

The great Hindu classic, the **Bhagavad Gita**, confirms this action of sacrifice and pain and that the Supreme Spirit is present in **all** action even that which is temporal. It says, '**All** action originates in the Supreme Spirit which is imperishable, and in sacrificial action the all-pervading Spirit is constantly present.' No man should ever premeditate the best way for himself. There is only one right way for each person and that is prepared for him according to his willingness, his temperament, sincerity, integrity and diligence. A man who is no athlete but desires to run like an athlete must first start on the many physical impediments which create the difference between him and the athlete. Sometimes the aspiring devotee is tempted to think about the ways and life of the monk, the hermit or the sage who sits at the top of the mountain devoting his life to meditation and he feels sad, even despondent, at his own inadequacies and earthly way of life. In which case he should take comfort from the following. **Every** way of life is directed by the Higher Self. To reject this thought is to reject the existence of the Higher Wisdom. Helped by certain aspects of Karmic law, particular circumstances and experiences are placed before the student to offer the best opportunities for spiritual development. Considering the position and ideals of the hermit on the mountain it may be much better and easier, thinks the student, to leap from a place of absolute peace and quiet through contemplation to a level of consciousness of the highest spiritual order; but it is a far greater achievement to find Christ in the busy rounds and actions of a bustling high street.

If we are seeking absolute enlightenment then it must be found, experienced and held on every level of consciousness, even the lowest. Wherever there is life there is no level on which the Absolute Self is not present. The devotee should also keep in mind that there is never, and can never be, only personal salvation. The Bible tells us 'Jesus wept.' He cried for the struggling millions of people steeped in ignorance and therefore suffering. The mystics themselves were totally inseparable from the same suffering. They realised that the suffering masses were totally incapable of helping themselves unless they came down to guide them to their level. As the mystic realised so must each devotee realise that the whole of one's life is a devotion not only to personal salvation but also to the struggling millions. Every human being is **one** soul and there are no 'fences' between souls of whatever nationality.

Let us again return to the question of the starting point within the ego-self. What can be of great value, which helps us to reach the Higher Self, but can only be achieved through action in the world of phenomena? As every action creates a reaction which we personally experience, then the answer to the above question must be knowledge, or more precisely, **self-knowledge**. The enlightened ones, or mystics, knew the way ahead because they realised and were part of the suffering of their brothers and sisters and were, therefore, able to show the way ahead. For us to know the way ahead for others we must first be knowledgeable regarding every aspect of ourselves. All of our actions are quite clearly the out-working on a material level of our deeper selves. In other words, our choice of action is the reflection of our 'soul-quality' including all desires and ambitions. We will never become aware of a cruel streak within us until we have created a cruel action and witnessed the reaction which would also demonstrate the pain and suffering we have created for the other. If there are seeds of greed, aggression, hate, lust and fear embedded within our souls we will remain ignorant of them until they flower in the action and we experience the reactions in others. On the other hand, the man who has seeds of love, compassion and understanding is not entangled in a world of selfish gain and his actions will reveal themselves as spiritual wisdom. But most people act because they desire something for themselves, they are attached to the 'fruits' of the action. Again we turn to the **Bhagavad Gita** for guidance on this chosen action, 'Do thy duty perfectly, without care for the **results**, for he who does his duty **disinterestedly** attains the supreme.' This is the reason why all scriptures teach us that every action should be committed with great understanding and realisation of the result, but with **de-tachment** from the 'fruits' of the action. The **Gita** again outlines this important lesson thus,

> 'In this world people are fettered by action, unless it is performed as a sacrifice [no fruits]. Therefore, O Arjuna, let thy acts be done without attachment, as sacrifice only. He who sees inaction in action, and action in inaction is the wisest of men. The wise call him a sage, for whatever he undertakes is free from the motives of desire, and his deeds are purified by the fire of wisdom. Having surrendered all claims to the

results of his actions, always contented and independent, in reality he does nothing even though he is apparently acting.'

So, this advice given to the devotee means that all your interest should be directed only to the deed itself without a thought for the results which may affect you. In other words, for any act to be spiritually effective it must be performed not for its own sake, but in the name of the Absolute Being, the inner spirit.

Now we are beginning to see that the starting point involves a form of discipline on the plane of matter, which, in truth, is the ego mind. First we become attached to the fruits of our actions, and the next stop is renunciation of the fruits of action. All actions of renunciation or sacrifice are a step forward. The movement of 'stepping forward' is wisdom or self-knowledge. This movement is likened to stepping out of a dark room into a lighted room. The light is only recognised and appreciated because of the first experience of darkness. Each single experience gives significance, or power, to the other. Therefore, if the opposite experience should not exist then the other has no power or significance. The act of renunciation should never be thought of as giving something up, or sacrificing something, it is expansion – spiritual expansion. The only thing we 'give up' is the desire, or illusion of the ego, but in truth we are actually expanding into the universal spirit or the experience of the unity of life. Of this the **Gita** says, 'He who experiences the unity of life sees his own Self in **all** beings, and all beings in him, and looks on everything with an impartial eye.'

The Way of Knowledge is the Way of Experience; which is to say experiencing the opposites. Many people make the mistake of believing that all knowledge comes **through** the mind. This is a serious error because there are numerous areas of truth or awareness which the mind cannot possibly reach but, at the same time, certain deeper parts of ourselves are in permanent contact. The outer mind is valuable when in pursuit of academic knowledge, but as a Way of Knowledge to the higher self it is seriously limited. Physicists and mathematicians tell us that time, space and material things, though valuable in one sense are useless in explaining the cosmic order. Our finite mind, or intellect, has its limited measure of creativity. Certain levels of thought, ideas and even emotions are free but free only to the extent they influence the phenomenal world.

Whilst there is no doubt that man's mind is the highest order of intelligence functioning in a terrestrial physical body, there is no evidence to show that man's mind is the highest order in the entire and vast evolutionary cycle of creation. On the contrary, when we consider the millions of different varieties of life, representing not only the infinite variety of forms but the infinite levels of consciousness, there can remain no doubt that an inventive and creative ingenuity of an infinite order is serving man's own evolution.

Many students of esoteric thought have encountered the words and works of a few whom we refer to as mystics. They talked of transient experiences, of glimpses of truth denoting a new dimension of consciousness. This consciousness has been given many names: Cosmic consciousness, mystical vision and inner reality, but they all mean the same thing and all constitute enlightenment. This very special kind of knowledge, these god-like potentialities which we have always had, but were simply lying dormant beneath numerous layers of veils, have to be achieved through an age-long process of descent into the deceiving darkness of materialism; this prison of illusion, where all sense of reality is lost followed by a slow, painful ascent during which self-knowledge, the consciousness of reality is gained, or shall we say, **re-gained**.

One of the clearest summaries of the process of enlightenment can be given by considering the tiny seed of a flower. If the seed is left lying in a place which is always dry, in the sunlight, in the warmth, it will remain always a seed. But the wise man places the seed in deep earth and total darkness. All conditions are negative – cold and damp isolation. The inherent qualities within the seed strive to overcome these unhappy conditions, perhaps instinctively knowing that above awaits the positive life and the light. Perhaps the negative and harsh forces of nature which lie below awaken the latent and unmanifest potentialities within urging them to overcome. From these latent forces emerge, climbing slowly inwards the light to become ultimately a beautiful flower. It is obvious to us all that the positive powers of sun and light alone could never have brought this beautiful creation about. Obviously, confinement, limitation and hindrance is an essential part of the cosmic plan to bring about the soul's progression. Somehow the cosmic law knew that by suppressing the vital essence or the soul's potentiality by ways of many veils (which may be called a body); by suppressing the complete awareness by means of sense-organs (constituting limitation), the real infinite values must overcome a prison which is finite and indecisive. This must be, and is, a vital principle, of life to which every variety of human, animal and plant life is subject. Not only must everything be credited to this principle but also every level of consciousness below the absolute. The acceptance of this principle gives a purpose to life, to the need for hindrance and limitation, and to illusion. It also gives intensity and passion to the soul, and a power and decisiveness, the absence of which would destroy all reason for living.

Those who find the vast cosmic process of descent into gross dark matter and the inevitable ascent to infinite light meaningless and unnecessary should remember that life is a constant, dynamic manifestation; it is not static. It is the absolute perfection of the infinite which **must** include finite possibilities. That which is complete, such as God, must also include the embryonic, otherwise how could we identify the complete, the absolute? The creativeness of the Absolute Consciousness must include embryonic, or simple, consciousness because it is in the **maturing** that they come to know their divinity; a divinity they have always had (it is their creator) but did not know they possessed. How can we possibly realise our infinity if first we do not know the finite? How can we come to the awareness of immortality if we do not first live believing we are mortal? Perfection without its opposite is static. Absolute beauty without its opposite is static. How can we come to know our true nature without a long process of descent through the many varying and complex levels which lie beneath the absolute? This process is the complete basis of the whole cycle of total enlightenment.

The slow descent into matter establishes the solid basis of egotism representing all knowledge pertaining to the nature and way of matter. It is this storehouse of information, facts and desires which establishes within the mind the idea that the phenomenal world it perceives is the realm of reality. It is the lowest stage which creates the sense of 'self', the 'I' and 'mine'. It is from this point that the rise to liberation begins. Edward Carpenter in his book **The Drama of Love and Death** gives a brilliant summary of the return:

> 'After the long descent and condensation and imprisonment of the spirit in its most limited and inert and self-regarding forms, after its saturation in matter, and its banishment in the world of death and suffering, the rising curve of liberation sets in, and the long process of its return. It is through love mainly that this second process works itself out. From point to point through unison with others by absorbing something from their experiences, by sharing a wider life the spirit's manifestation grows. Each soul is a gradual rising to consciousness to the All-Soul, a gradual liberation and self-discovery of the divine germ within it.'

For the reader to understand and accept the whole process of 'becoming' he must realise that all aspects of matter and every level of consciouness from the lowest embodies the divine germ even though much condensed. All life stems from this vital source. It is the active principle and it is constantly expressing the lesson of grossness, separation and illusion. Now begins the whole process of a slow progressive elimination of the illusions engendered by the soul's imprisonment in passive matter. The divine germ, like an embryo entombed in the womb of matter, must emerge and escape by its own activity, and disengage itself totally from the passive principle - matter.

We started this chapter by asking the question, 'What benefit can be achieved through the ego's association with the material world, at the same time realising that the ego, itself, cannot achieve reality? It is easy to use words, terms and analogies to try to answer this question but, quite obviously, we are attempting to explain something that is totally beyond the normal intellect. Therefore it is to be expected that only clues or thoughts from meditation can be offered with the hope they will point you in the direction in which you may find the truth. An enlightened person always thinks from the centre never from the periphery, but first he must know where the centre is and he can only know that by understanding the periphery. To put it another way, reason is of the mind, truth is beyond the reasoning mind but in order to get beyond the mind we must first know mind. Therefore, to become truth enlightened, something irrational is needed, something beyond reason. God is beyond reason we cannot prove God. In attempting to prove God you have missed the truth completely. Masters and mystics do not prove God because they **know** they **are** God. Mystics and masters say 'We are absurd because we belong not to this world of sense, we belong to something that lies beyond.' Therefore that which is beyond is bound to be of 'no-sense'. Whatever you can make sense of belongs to the world of methods, systems, ideas, beliefs and reasons. God and Truth are not methods, beliefs or ideas. These are things that surround you. They go round and round. Through reason and sense you keep on moving, but moving around a circle, never getting anywhere, staying on the same spot.

Masters and mystics have stopped moving in a circle. They are out of the wheel. They are aware of that which is beyond reason and beyond sense. Once the vicious circle stops – God is there. The master is still in this world but not **of** it. Masters never imitate, or follow (as most of us do) Jesus, Buddha or Krishna because they **are** what they are. But, on the other hand, they are aware of these great teachers. People use gurus and teachers to find liberation, but what happens is that they create a bondage. Buddha says, 'Be a light unto **yourself**.' He instructed the seekers to stand in **the middle**. If you stay in the middle you cannot move into the extremes. If you stay away from the extremes the mind disappears, that mind which is a collection of ideas, methods, beliefs, information and systems.

The middle way is the only way to truth, to the Absolute Self. The Absolute Self is not an extreme. It is neither left nor right. It is not a pathway of coming or going. But to **become** the middle first we must recognise and for a time believe ourselves to be independent of the extremes. The ego-self provides us with these experiences; experiences which, though temporal, like the ego, are vital and necessary to help us to recognise and understand the nature of the extremes. Only in this way do we recognise, the become, the middle way. This then is the starting point and the vital benefit we receive through the ego's association with the material world. The real purpose of man's existence is to fashion the **real** out of that which is unreal. In truth we are saying:

> The unreal is the **promise** of the Real
> Darkness is the overshadowing of Light
> Death is the gateway to Life and Immortality
> In the unreal He helps us to find the Real
> In darkness He helps us to find the Light
> In death enables us to perceive Immortality.

CHAPTER TEN

COMMON PROBLEMS TO PROGRESSION

The problems confronting the soul are so colossal, so complex that to understand and overcome them so that the soul may progress we must approach each of our activities in a fully conscious and direct manner. Solutions will never be found in the **outside** circumstances even though many other people are also closely involved. The solutions are not to be found by changing your environment, your job, neighbours, friends or teachers. Solutions are to be found only in the mind of their creator. The same mind that creates fear, suspicion, misunderstanding, hatred and greed.

It always **appears** that our worries and problems originate from conditions and people of the outside world. The truth is that the outside world is incapable of creating anything. They merely reflect the inadequacies and weaknesses of our own mind. The outside world is **our** relationship with all things and other people. The world with its collection of things and other people cannot, in any possible way, be separated from us. The world, the society, the community, the family is the relationship **we** create and with it we also create the conditions by our mental attitudes and responses.

So, the world around us is not the problem, we are the problem. We are the cause and the effect. The world, our immediate environment and our relationship with it, are a projection of ourselves. We cannot separate ourselves from the world's problems because the world's problems are our problems. If it were possible totally to separate ourselves from the world we would only suffer stagnation. We become affected and motivated by many of the world's, or the community's, problems so worry, fear, happiness and joy are created in the mind. We cannot transform the world, or the community, by worrying and hoping that the **leaders** will change their ways or policies. This is foolish and negative thinking. We can never change the quality of the souls of others by worrying about their actions and thoughts. We must start with ourselves. There are basically two worlds. The outer world with its five thousand million people all acting independently, and our own inner world. We have no control whatsoever over the outer world, but we have total control over our inner world. Conflicts are only created when we lose control over our inner world. When there is conflict on the outside and loss of control on the inside then we have all-round conflicts and wars. Therefore, to transform the world each soul must begin with itself. We must begin with our motives. We start by attempting to understand the nature of ourselves, never making the mistake of thinking that mistakes and problems are the responsibilities of other persons or other groups. If their actions are affecting you in any way, then the problems are very much yours. Never be a Pontius Pilate and wash your hands of the problems of others because if they are disturbing you then you are an inseparable part of the same conflict.

So we must try to discover the way of understanding ourselves. The way is not by deciding to 'keep yourself to yourself'. You cannot withdraw from the world. Isolation is stagnation. No one can live or progress in isolation. To find the right way we must be related, for to be without relationship is to be in isolation. Problems, conflicts and misery arise not only because of the wrong relationship, but because of the lack of relationship. Remember, it takes two angry people to create an argument. When there is one placid, controlled person and one angry person there is no conflict. If we can transform our own character by inner control it will act like the ever-widening ring of ripples in a pool of water.

What is it within us that creates conflicts? Well, begin by imagining your soul resembling a balloon filled with clear liquid. Suspended within the liquid are a large number of black and white particles. The black particles represent areas of ignorance and self-attachment. Mystics refer to them as areas of 'unknowing': These are the creations of the ego-mind. They are the centres from which possessiveness, pride, dignity and authority originate. They are the 'I' or 'Mine' aspect. The white particles are the areas of 'knowing'; the areas of spiritual awareness. They are the centres of love, compassion, tolerance, kindness and truth. The 'quality' of soul consciousness is decided by the 'weight' of black areas when compared with the number of white areas. If the white areas are greater, then we have an evolving soul.

Both black and white particles are the 'sensors' of the soul. Our relationship with the world is the only means whereby we can bring about a soul transformation or revolution. Real revolution is actually a **revolution of values**. That means, the composition of black and white soul areas constitutes a value. By reducing the number of black areas we improve the soul value. It is a revolutionary change in sensually affected areas which transforms them into areas which are not created by environmental or personal influences.

To bring about this transformation it is essential that we begin by getting to know ourselves. Self-knowledge is the beginning of self-wisdom. So we begin by noticing how the behaviour of others affects us physically, verbally and mentally, bearing in mind that anger, aggression and all acts of conflict are mere reflections, or reactions of our inner areas of 'unknowing'; in other words a black soul particle. Every time we react to another's action with anger or aggression, whether it be physical, verbal or only by thought, that outer action has clearly indicated an area of ignorance within. Once again it reveals that the problem lies within ourselves. Therefore, the so-called difficult person has, in truth, acted as a kind of teacher towards us.

Let me put this particular lesson, or truth, to you in another way. Supposing you are suffering a physical pain. The obvious thing to do is visit your doctor. After his examination of your body he discloses the fact that you have a disease. You may display fear and anxiety, but you would never be angry with the doctor because you will recognise the fact that he has done you a valuable service by disclosing that you have a problem. In this particularly skilled way he will ultimately deal with the discomfort. The ways of the physician are generally understood and accepted with gratitude. If we are to know ourselves as we actually are and not as we think we are, we must be prepared courageously and honestly to recognise all the faults we have in the soul. The only way to do this is to note and recognise our reactions to another's actions. An angry, aggressive reaction clearly denotes that they have uncovered a problem **within you**, an area of ignorance. The other person may not be a physician but you can think of him as your **spiritual doctor**.

Now is the time to take careful note of your reaction. Why did you get angry or irritated? Was your pride, dignity or sense of authority damaged? All these reactions stem from the ego-mind. It is important to recognise and note these things because, though self-knowledge cannot be given to us by others, they, or their effect upon us, are the only means by which we can realise the faults within ourselves. Always remember that these faults are the same faults as in other people. Therefore, in other people we can see ourselves.

To acquire self-knowledge there must be an extraordinary alertness of mind which must be totally free from self-deception. It is the most difficult decision of all for one to admit that he is greedy, deceitful, envious and aggressive. It is all too easy to find excuses for one's behaviour. Nonetheless, recognising and accepting the real nature of your character is the beginning of virtue. To understand and benefit from the process there must be a determined and honest intention to know your true character which will call for critical observation and analysis of every thought, feeling and action.

The mind will be quick to make reasonable excuses for angry thoughts and violent action provoked by the aggressive attitude of another. In such a situation the ego-mind suddenly and angrily thrusts forward the thought that there are justifiable reasons for taking retaliatory counter-action. This of course is wrong and totally destructive not only to yourself, but also to the other person. All that happens is that the situation has been unnecessarily aggravated and nothing constructive has been achieved. To understand yourself it is also necessary to understand the thoughts and the actions of the other person. So it may come about, because of your impulsive counter-action, that you have avenged yourself on the other person because you believed you were justified.

Now consider this. Was it the 'area' of your consciousness which demanded retaliatory action of a spiritual nature or was it of the ego-mind? If you have resolved to be honest with yourself then obviously you will agree it was of an un-spiritual nature. Now let us consider this situation a little further. After the so-called 'justifiable' act was committed, did the unspiritual area dissolve or did it remain with you? The answer is an obvious one. The unspiritual area remains with you because an unspiritual act cannot dissolve itself nor can it create a spiritual area. Only love, compassion, understanding and tolerance can do that. An unspiritual thought is still creative but it can only create that of its own nature which may be expressed as words or physical action. The removal, or death, of the person who has offended you will not solve your problem because there will always be a thousand other irritating persons ready to take their place. It cannot be emphasised enough that the problem lies not in the other person but within yourself. There should always arise in your consciousness the question, 'Is this the right thing or not?' And when the true answer comes there should also arise the answer, 'My most difficult neighbour is also my finest teacher.' If every soul could hold and treasure this thought then the world about us would be transformed. But in order to transform the world with its wars, misery, starvation, class distinction and confusion, the transformation must always begin with oneself. It can never be left to your neighbour or to the other party because you cannot transform your neighbour without transforming yourself.

To bring about a fundamental revolution in oneself, one must thoroughly understand the entire process of one's thoughts and feelings in **all** relationships. This is the one and only solution, not only to the world's problems, but also to our own. It is entirely useless to seek the help of more teachers, more disciples, more beliefs, more ideologies and more methods. If we can begin to understand ourselves as we are from moment to moment, from thought to thought, from act to act there will surely develop a subtle state of tranquillity. Only from that state of tranquillity can there be spiritual creativeness.

To summarise, if the nature of man does not in some degree become involved in, and reflect, something of the ultimate levels, how can he know anything of them at all? If he cannot discover divinity within himself, where in the realms of the universe and in the spiritual levels shall he look with any hope of success? All problems of the universe and of the nature of knowledge, therefore, come back to man himself, and in doing so throw light upon himself. The Tao Te Ching said, 'He who knows others is wise but he who knows himself is enlightened.'

Problems in Daily Action

Thought is action. The quality of the action is related to the quality of the consciousness. Each individual is inescapably involved in a series of actions. Even should the body be completely incapable of physical movement, thought is action. Many of the actions may be considered seemingly unrelated to a specific cause. Some actions lead to frustration, anger, anxiety and even aggression. Actions, whether distressing or enjoyable, involve every human soul, in fact every living, mobile form which includes animals and birds, because without action there cannot be life, there cannot be any thinking, no reactions only stagnation.

Every producer of action, be it human or animal, is inevitably caught up in the reaction which is inescapable. To thrust our hand into a pail of boiling water, whether accidently or deliberately, instantly produces a painful reaction. We may suffer greatly, but the element of surprise never comes into the mind because we understand the whole **process** of the action and reaction. Only a very young baby would be surprised at the reaction, simply because it would be ignorant of the **process**. To be caught up in the outward action and the reaction without understanding the **whole** process of action always leads to frustration, depression, a sense of injustice and even aggression.

Living, and therefore thinking, consists of an endless process of action at different levels of consciousness. Consider the vast difference between the consciousness of a mystic or sage and that of a cold arrogant egocentric, then one will realise how extreme are the different levels of consciousness. The same measure can be equally applied to the great difference between the intellectual levels and the inspirationally artistic levels. We have Pythagoras, Plato, Einstein, Empedocles and many others on one hand and Michelangelo, Leonardo da Vinci, Mozart, Chopin, Tennyson, Rossetti, Browning and others on the other hand. Then somewhere in this vast scale of differences we must place the intellect of the primitive tribesmen of Africa and the interiors of Australia. These infinite levels of consciousness are so complex that they are far beyond understanding by the mind. To understand them one can only approach them in a simple direct manner, that is by experiencing each act and reaction as they manifest daily. The understanding can only be realised by the creator of the acts when their awareness and self-analysis realises the **quality** of their reactions.

Consciousness is **experiencing**, recognising and giving significance, or value, to every act and reaction. Every value is then committed to the memory bank. This entire process **is** action. Consciousness is action and each item of action must be thought of as a kind of challenge to the outside world. It can be a spiritual or earthly challenge, but whatever it is, some kind of response is always expected. The response is the **experiencing** whether it is good, bad or painful. Each and every response is telling us something about ourselves and that something concerns the quality of consciousness which prompted the initial act. The reader should now consider that without challenge, without experiencing, without recording the response (which is memory) there can be no 'educational' reaction.

Action creates and reflects the true character of the person. The character comes into being when action initiates a reaction or result. In other words, the committed action **must** have an end or result in view. Therefore action, reaction and anticipated result is a unitary process which means a single and complete process. To achieve a particular result means that first there must be desire. For example, 'I want to be a rich man'. 'I want a new car', 'I want to be well known', 'I want promotion', 'I want more money' and so on. The desire has a **quality** meaning which originates in a particular level of consciousness. The vital purpose of all action is to achieve **something**, but the end, after many false starts, numerous illusionary and negative results, the soul finally comes to the realisation that the only real achievement is self-knowledge, or self-realisation. This is the only foundation upon which we can commence the process of **becoming**, or enlightenment.

When we examine the normal process of our daily life we eventually come to the conclusion that it consists of three major states. There is the **thought**, then the **action**, followed by the end **result**. These three states constitute **experience**, which is also our daily existence, but it is also the process of development. Let us suppose that there is no action, therefore no result, no experience. Then there cannot be any progress so it is reasonable to suppose that every kind of action, negative and positive, is important to the soul's development. The whole of our daily life is simply a process of becoming **something**. If we believe ourselves to be ignorant then we want to become wise or learned. If we are sickly, we want to become strong and healthy. If we are poor, we want to become financially well off. When we have sufficiently experienced every aspect of materiality we, by instinct, would want to become more aware of the spirituality within. So, in other words, our whole life is devoted to **becoming** something. The power behind the urge to become something is the Will. Now this urge to become something must, inevitably, involve some kind of effort or struggle because it involves the potent thought, **'I am that now, but I want to become something better'**. The process of **becoming** must involve pain, struggle, conflict and anxiety. Each lower state (what you are now) must prompt a challenge. From this there must come a reaction, or response, followed by the recognition of the experience which will be memorised. This process can be felt at different levels of consciousness. This is the constant, but necessary, struggle of progression. So the situation is this, if there is no action and no reaction there cannot be evolvement.

Thus the problem of life is that the person creates action because he has an object or end view in mind. Usually, action is created by an idea but if the idea originates from a materialistic level of consciousness then this must, in time, create anxiety, frustration and even anger, because the source is not permanent. Now let us try to analyse the value, if any, of this frustrating experience. Let us say you experience anger, hate or fear. During the actual **experiencing** you are not aware of yourself as a person, there is only the state of **experiencing**. Hence the statement, 'He was not thinking of what he was doing', or, 'I did not realise what I was doing'. Immediately after the experience, that is when the actual experiencing has ceased, you become conscious of yourself. The reaction could be one of remorse, shame, embarrassment, foolishness or even satisfaction if the motive had been revenge. At that moment we have recognised and recorded the nature of the reaction, which must be accepted as being of the same quality as the original action. All human life is a process of becoming something else, something better. The desire to **be** something else is the **will to become** which means more action, or effort, to achieve a different level of living or consciousness.

To realise with regret your state of anger, aggression, hate or greediness after a particular action, or reaction, reveals a subtle desire for a different and better end or result. This emergence of the 'will to be' prepares the way for the 'will to become'. Therefore the problem we have to face is that there must be action (at different levels) to prepare for the 'becoming' but there cannot be action without pain, without effort, without conflict. There must always remain ahead of us the object, the end-view, the will. To sum up, the 'I am this and I want to become that' **is** strife, **is** pain, **is** constant struggle. Therefore if there is no object, no action, no reaction there is no enlightenment.

During the actual experiencing, the 'self' is lost, there is only the experience of anger, hate, etc., which is followed by the realisation of the nature of the experience. The realisation may reveal ugly, disturbing sides to our nature, but, fortunately, out of this conflict arises an object, or end-view, to resolve not to allow anger and aggression to arise again. As it happens we find ourselves in this stage again and again. But we always overcome it and resolve again and again to prevent it from happening next time. Nonetheless, each experience is recognised and recorded and the will to resolve is repeated. This is continuity of action and reaction which eventually leads to enlightenment, because each action brings further understanding of the fundamental nature of ourselves.

If we can understand the nature of action in the basic sense, that is in all its lower forms, then that fundamental understanding will ultimately bring about an awareness of slightly higher forms and so the slow process of **becoming** goes on. It is much like a person who has always had a burning ambition to own a motor car but because of financial problems could not afford one. Then one day he manages to get an old, very much worn-out car. At first he is excited, happy and satisfied. But as time goes on and the initial excitement dies, he yearns for a better car of a more attractive appearance. So the process goes on until one day he becomes the owner of an extremely handsome motor car. This is a simple example of the will, the object, or end-view, the action and the continuity of becoming. Action is the mere tool of the thought or idea. Ideas breed further improved ideas, and this process applies not only to the physical level but every level of consciousness right up to the highest spiritual levels.

All ideas, actions and reaction are the result of a **past** experience. A past experience becomes a part of the memory bank. Therefore, an idea or thought could be the result of stored up memories of past experiences. At a later time certain circumstances and encounters will develop when the memory bank will produce a related idea, a thought, or action. The encounter (or circumstances) cause an action prompted by the memory of past experience. Therefore the action or response is **already** conditioned by the memory. Do not forget, memory always belongs to the past. So in such a situation always bring to mind the thought that your present action could be the response of something that has long since been dead.

An action, or response based upon this thought process is a hindrance to enlightenment. The past is dead unless you make a bondage out of it, unless you have become a slave to the past. What happened in the past, no matter how bad, can, however, be your teacher and your liberator. The past is your only doorway to liberty, providing you open the door and leave the room which houses the dead experiences. The past is there to liberate you. Love is action. Love is not based upon an idea or thought. Love is not memory based upon past experience. Hate is based upon past experience.

Love is not based upon experience or memory. Love is action but there is no separation between love and action as there is between idea (thought) and action. Love is liberation, forgiveness and tolerance. Compassion is liberation. Love is never the outcome or result of a past experience; it is not an idea. Hate, resentment and aggression are the result of past experience; they are based upon ideas.

If we want enlightenment, if we want liberation from fear, frustration, anxiety and stagnation we must start by bringing about a radical change in ourselves. We commence by making a tremendous effort to control the action of past habits and past ideas. We must learn to resist the habitual responses of past experiences. Our whole life is based upon effort in order to achieve some particular result. Sooner or later we must come to the realisation that all effort, which is made from the centre of the ego-mind, must inevitably result in more conflict, more frustration, more misery which means we have to keep on creating more and more effort. For example the effort of obtaining a beefburger for lunch does not clear up all our problems connected with future lunches. On the contrary, we have to continue with the efforts and, at times, even increase them. So our misery increases, our anxieties and fears increase. We have achieved nothing except ideas for future unending efforts. Still we keep on and on hoping that in some fortunate way things will get better.

Though a beefburger is necessary to maintain the body, troubles, conflicts, fears and anxieties only arise when we put all our faith, hope and thought into nothing else but a beefburger. It is totally impossible for the body to progress. Only the soul progresses. True, we have a duty to our body but we also have an equal duty to our soul. We cannot ignore one or the other, otherwise there is misery and conflict. Buddha says always stay on the middle way. Mind only stays in the **extremes**. Love is in the mind. Hate is in the mind. The negative is in the mind. The positive is in the mind. In the middle there are no ideas, no past experiences. Because the mind holds love and hate, doubt and trust, ignorance and wisdom, fear and peace. They are the extremes.

Try to live by simply standing in the middle. If you stand in the middle the mind disappears because you are not fluctuating between the extremes. To understand the reality and significance of life we must try to understand what is meant by not 'fluctuating' between the extremes or opposites. Fluctuation means effort, what does effort mean? Surely, effort means a series of attempts to change the present state into something that does not yet exist. Is this not an admission that we are dissatisfied or unhappy with the present state? Does this signify fear, boredom, frustration, desire, greed or ambition, the signs of a discontented man? What creates discontent? Only the mind of attachment. The truly contented man is he who fully recognises the value and the significance of the present state. The mind cannot do this because it is only concerned with how few or how many possessions it has, the worry about getting more or the fear of losing what it has.

The contented man is aware of the difference between reality (spirit) and illusion (material attachment). Let us take a brief look at some aspects of reality. For instance, can you struggle to be happy? Can one decide or make an effort to be in love? Is there joy, inspiration or intuition in effort? We can suppress some things, sacrifice and control others, but happiness and joy do not come through sacrifice, suppression or control. When you think about it our entire life is a series of suppressions, sacrifices and controls. A constant struggle with our desires, ambitions, emotions, passions and your selfish, greedy instincts. We indulge in all these efforts in the hope that we will find happiness, security and peace of mind. Alas, the series of efforts never stop. Life is a constant desire to overcome, a constant struggle with our desires. Yet, do love and compassion develop from struggle, strife and effort?

Effort, which is usually a self-centred activity, is a refusal to accept what the situation really is. A refusal to recognise that the situation we are trying to transform is the situation we created in the first place. Our social, economic and environmental situation is the result of our activities in the past. In the past we have striven to achieve results. We strived to transform that which was already in being, without realising that we had already created it. Our mind and thought was the creator.

We get married in an effort to change our life. Love, however, is a spontaneous thing. We cannot strive for it, we cannot think about it and so bring it into being. It just happens during a time when we are completely free of the mind. The decision to marry is not always free from the mind. Very often there are reasons such as physical attraction, domination, ambition, financial security, loneliness or boredom; each, in a way, is exploiting the other's assets. Once people are married love becomes a recognisable bond, a form of possession. Slowly, bit by bit, all the make-up of courtship disappears. Then the real person appears and there are many clashes. Gradually, love disappears; it disappears because real love was never there in the first place. Real love is the most eternal thing in the world; it cannot disappear. Everything of the mind, of the material world can disappear, but not love. Love is the complete expression of the eternal self – it is the eternal phenomenon.

Love of the mind always disappears in time because you were trying to transform yourself, your environment and circumstances for **reasons** – reasons of the mind. Everything of the outside we attempt to transform because of reason must be of a temporal nature. We waste too much time trying to transform ourselves and the longer we spend fooling ourselves the greater become the burdens and the conflicts. We are all actors pretending to be some other character. If we try to be an actor for twenty-four hours a day, we feel confined, imprisoned. We develop a tense state of mind. As the confinement continues we become frustrated. We create plans – which are reasons – to break out. Unfortunately, we do not know the right direction. We should be breaking **inwardly**. Burdens and conflicts increase, which are sometimes impossible to live with. The state of mind creates false ideas, it begins to blame other people. So the mind reacts and seeks revenge by way of angry outbursts, suspicions, aggression, and even hatred. Therefore, if love, marriage and reason is just a means of achieving something else then it will never achieve a truly happy existence. We fail if we seek self-fulfilment in an object, in an ambition, in a person, or in an idea because to hold on to that achievement demands constant effort and struggle.

Why is there always this desire to fulfil ourselves? Is it because of the awareness that we are lacking in something, or we do not have enough of something. We may feel we are lacking in position, ambition self-esteem, confidence, power, finance, authority or recognition. To fill that void constitutes the whole process of our existence, with the result that we create ideas, plans and efforts to collect these things **outwardly.** In truth we are trying to run away from our own deficiences. Our deficiences are a state of **mind**. We sense an **inward poverty**, and we are trying to escape from this inner void, little realising that we cannot fill this inner void with outward things. If it is futile to run away from the inner poverty, what is the answer? We feel, if we do nothing, we are stagnating. We become forlorn, helpless and lost. We feel without effort life has become useless.

Now let us consider a creative way out of this dilemma. We start with ourselves. No one has the power to create conflicts or miseries for us unless we first give them the power. In other words we create our own problems. Outward effort exists only as long as we consider escape from our deficiencies and lack of possessions. But when we courageously look at the situation, consider it, analyse it and totally accept it without any excuse or thought of avoidance, and then consider the real nature, not only of our escape, but of the reason and the end product, there slowly develops a state of mind in which all strife and anxiety ceases. That state of being is contemplative creativeness and it is the very opposite of strife, effort, reason and desire.

Whenever we try truly to understand the real nature of our efforts, our reasons and our inadequacies there arises a creative spiritual reality, a spiritual intelligence which gradually opens the way to enlightenment and happiness.

Therefore, to sum up: action on the outward plane is the enemy. Action means continuous reaction. It is the mind's way of refusing to look at the reality of the situation. Buddha says, 'In no-thing will you find the truth.' When the mind is free of reason, free from the desire for action, free from thoughts of inadequacy, free from the awareness of your outer state, then this is the **action** of the creative being. Always observe your outward thoughts and actions. Observe and analyse the end-product. Is it a beefburger? When you understand the nature and purpose of the beefburger you understand the nature, the purpose and illusion of all 'things'.

Only in this way will you acquire self-knowledge - through constant awareness the knowledge that all reasons, ideas and end-views are endless battles going on around you. Try to become aware of the **inward** inadequacies. Resolve to live with them, to recognise them without thought of escape then you will know happiness and security.